the twilight saga
new moon

THE OFFICIAL ILLUSTRATED MOVIE COMPANION

BY MARK COTTA VAZ

www.atombooks.co.uk

ATOM

Copyright © 2009 by Little, Brown and Company
Unless otherwise credited, all photographs copyright © 2009 by Summit Entertainment, LLC

The moral right of the author has been asserted.

All characters and events in this publication, other than those
clearly in the public domain, are fictitious and any resemblance
to real persons, living or dead, is purely coincidental.

All rights reserved.
No part of this publication may be reproduced, stored in a
retrieval system, or transmitted, in any form or by any means, without
the prior permission in writing of the publisher, nor be otherwise circulated
in any form of binding or cover other than that in which it is published
and without a similar condition including this condition being
imposed on the subsequent purchaser.

A CIP catalogue record for this book
is available from the British Library.

First Atom UK edition 2009
Reprinted 2009, twice

Book design by Georgia Rucker Design

ISBN 978-1-905654-68-0

Printed and bound in the UK by Butler Tanner & Dennis Ltd, Frome

Atom
An imprint of
Little, Brown Book Group
100 Victoria Embankment
London EC4Y 0DY

An Hachette UK Company
www.hachette.co.uk

www.atombooks.co.uk

To Stephenie Meyer and Chris Weitz, the cast and crew who brought *New Moon* to life, and to my favorite Twilighters: Katelin Vaz Labat and recent convert Teresa Vaz Goodfellow. You all shine in the light. . .

—M.C.V.

A round of applause and a grand huzzah for the talented *The Twilight Saga: New Moon* filmmakers, whose memories and insights into the production inform this book:

CHRIS WEITZ, DIRECTOR

MELISSA ROSENBERG, SCREENWRITER

DAVID BRISBIN, PRODUCTION DESIGNER

CATHERINE IRCHA, ART DIRECTOR

JAVIER AGUIRRESAROBE, DIRECTOR OF PHOTOGRAPHY

PETER LAMBERT, EDITOR

ABRAHAM FRASER, LOCATION MANAGER

RENE HAYNES, CASTING

TISH MONAGHAN, COSTUME DESIGNER

THOM MCINTYRE, KEY HAIRSTYLIST

NORMA HILL-PATTON, KEY MAKEUP

J.J. MAKARO, STUNT COORDINATOR

SUSAN MACLEOD, VISUAL EFFECTS SUPERVISOR AND PRODUCER

ERIC PASCARELLI, VISUAL EFFECTS SUPERVISOR, PRIME FOCUS

TIPPETT STUDIO, *NEW MOON* TEAM

PHIL TIPPETT, VISUAL EFFECTS SUPERVISOR

MATT JACOBS, CO-VISUAL EFFECTS SUPERVISOR

NATE FREDENBURG, ART DIRECTOR

TOM GIBBONS, ANIMATION SUPERVISOR

KEN KOKKA, VISUAL EFFECTS PRODUCER

KIP LARSEN, EXECUTIVE PRODUCER

WYCK GODFREY, PRODUCER

BILL BANNERMAN, LINE PRODUCER

GILLIAN BOHRER, DIRECTOR OF DEVELOPMENT, SUMMIT ENTERTAINMENT

ANDI ISAACS, EXECUTIVE VICE PRESIDENT AND HEAD OF PHYSICAL PRODUCTION, SUMMIT ENTERTAINMENT

ERIK FEIG, PRESIDENT OF PRODUCTION AND ACQUISITIONS, SUMMIT ENTERTAINMENT

I had a secret

that wasn't mine to tell, yet a secret I felt bound to protect. A secret, that suddenly, he seemed to know all about.[1]

TABLE OF CONTENTS

INTRODUCTION

THESE VIOLENT DELIGHTS HAVE VIOLENT ENDS AND IN THEIR TRIUMPH DIE, LIKE FIRE AND POWDER, WHICH, AS THEY KISS, CONSUME.

—ROMEO AND JULIET, ACT II, SCENE VI

With this quote from Shakespeare's immortal tale of star-crossed young lovers, Stephenie Meyer opened the door to NEW MOON, her follow-up novel to TWILIGHT. The words are from Friar Laurence to Romeo, spoken as the two await Juliet's arrival for a secret marriage ceremony, which the friar has agreed to perform. Laurence's prescient fear echoes Romeo's defiant words about his beloved:

Then love-devouring death do what he dare,
It is enough I may but call her mine.

Like Shakespeare's doomed lovers, Edward Cullen and Bella Swan are heedless of "love-devouring death" and the chasm between them—Edward, a vampire and forever seventeen, is in love with mortal Bella who, with her eighteenth birthday approaching, would happily become a vampire if only Edward would relent and change her. Despite reaching this impasse, TWILIGHT concludes with the two exchanging declarations of undying love.

In NEW MOON, Edward leaves Bella. As she laments in the novel, "I was like a lost moon—my planet destroyed in some cataclysmic, disaster-movie scenario of desolation— that continued, nevertheless, to circle in a tight little orbit around the empty space left behind, ignoring the laws of gravity." [2]

This heartbreak is only the beginning of Bella's emotional journey. In NEW MOON she discovers that life goes on, that others can become precious to her—and that everlasting love might be possible after all.

In her time of darkness, the supernatural realms open up even wider than the comfortable confines of the Cullen house where she truly began her initiation into things normally unseen by mortals. Shape-shifting creatures prowl the ancient forests of her Pacific Northwest home, and even her experience with vampires—mostly with the genteel Cullens, "vegetarian vampires" who do not feast on human blood—pales in the light of the larger ancient world that seems waiting, as if preordained, to claim her.

In *Twilight* Time

Robert Pattinson as Edward Cullen and Kristen Stewart as Bella Swan.

It has passed into *Twilight* lore, the freezing cold, snow, sleet, and rain that battered the movie production crew laboring to adapt Stephenie Meyer's first novel in locations that matched the book's Olympic Peninsula forest setting. The goal was to be faithful to the book right down to its locations, and Meyer's story was set in the real town of Forks, Washington. It's the rainiest spot in the continental United States and thus perfect for vampires blending into human society. In Meyer's mythology, vampires are not nocturnal (in fact, they never sleep), but their skin reacts to sunlight with a dazzling luminosity. Instead of shooting in isolated Forks, the production filmed in and around Portland, Oregon. It was one of the worst winters in years, and even the last day of shooting was marked by heavy rain. As director Catherine Hardwicke reported in her online production diary: "Principal photography is ending…we survived

snow, hail, sleet, torrential downpours, and blazing sun (when we didn't want it)—sometimes all in one day. SEVERE WEATHER is an understatement."3

The production was a high-stakes project for Summit Entertainment, a company that had specialized in foreign distribution and cofinancing of film projects, and was making the move into full-scale production. Summit secured rights to TWILIGHT in December 2006 and completed the acquisition of the book rights in June 2007. The *Twilight* film was to be the flagship project for the fledgling studio headquartered in Santa Monica, California. Both studio and filmmakers were confident, feeling the wave of a phenomenon carrying them along.

"We always thought *Twilight* could be a success at the level we needed it to be successful, [based upon] the audience of girls and women who bought the books," noted producer Wyck Godfrey who,

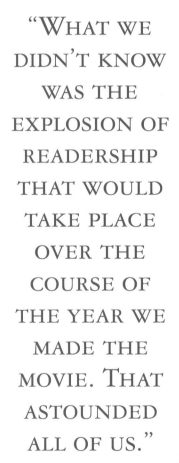

"WHAT WE DIDN'T KNOW WAS THE EXPLOSION OF READERSHIP THAT WOULD TAKE PLACE OVER THE COURSE OF THE YEAR WE MADE THE MOVIE. THAT ASTOUNDED ALL OF US."

with executive producer Karen Rosenfelt, was among the *Twilight* veterans returning for *The Twilight Saga: New Moon*. "What we didn't know was the explosion of readership that would take place over the course of the year we made the movie. That astounded all of us. There were hints while we were making it, particularly the fans being on location and wanting to catch a glimpse of filming."

TWILIGHT is something special and intensely personal to the fans. They have become kindred spirits in the unfolding drama of the mortal teenager in love with a vampire, a fervor that heated up as Edward and Bella became physically incarnated for the movie adaptation and fans awaited the November 21, 2008, release of *Twilight*.

The touchstone moment for producer Wyck Godfrey came when Kristen Stewart (Bella), Robert Pattinson (Edward), and Taylor

The New Moon *cast appeared at a* Twilight *screening during the 2009 Comic-Con International show in San Diego, California.*

Lautner (Jacob Black) stepped onto the stage at the 2008 Comic-Con International convention in San Diego, an annual event and mecca for American popular culture. At the Summit Entertainment panel, which featured *Twilight* the movie, "it was…shrill," Godfrey laughed. "The noise from the fans was drowning out every other auditorium. A director friend of

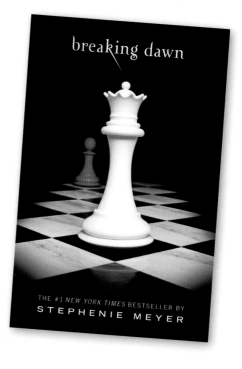

TWILIGHT IS SOMETHING SPECIAL AND INTENSELY PERSONAL TO THE FANS.

mine was doing a presentation at the same time and he told me he couldn't get his words out, it was so loud in our auditorium. The power of the franchise bleeding out into the public consciousness took place there."

Serendipitously, Stephenie Meyer's own literary profile was raised with the release of her first adult market novel, THE HOST, adding to the anticipation of the theatrical release of *Twilight*. By summer of 2008, the fourth and final volume of her saga arrived with the midnight release of BREAKING DAWN. The confluence of factors roiling the pop zeitgeist confounded box-office expectations. "The audience for the movie was growing every month leading up to the film's release," Godfrey recalled. "The tracking kept going up—we could do $30 million in the weekend,

then it was $40 to $50 million, and by Friday—holy cow!—we're going to do $70 million."

Reportedly the highest grossing opening ever for a female director, the film was on its way to a global box-office haul of over $380 million. Stewart, Pattinson, and other cast members became overnight celebrities, subjects of slick magazine cover articles and glossy photo spreads. Their public appearances became wild happenings, while the intrigues of filmmaking—would actor Taylor Lautner return as Bella's friend, Jacob?—became obsessions on Internet blogs and fan sites.

In the immediate aftermath of the movie, enraptured fans were clamoring to see NEW MOON on the big screen. The studio was way ahead of them—even while Catherine Hardwicke was in postproduction work on *Twilight*, Summit had already given *Twilight* screenwriter Melissa Rosenberg the assignment to write the sequel. Then, with good news at the box office, a *New Moon* production was greenlit "the first business day after the opening of *Twilight*," noted Erik Feig, Summit's president of production and acquisitions.

"The initial challenge in making *Twilight* was to make a movie that would vaguely echo the movie playing in millions of people's minds as they were reading the book," Feig explained. "People accepted it, not as a replacement for the book, but they liked our version of Edward and Bella, as well as the Edward and Bella they had cast in their heads. *Twilight* had to get across a sense of love at first sight, and that's what Catherine was able to get across. The challenge for *New Moon* was, how do we get across the sense of abandonment and heartbreak? It's a more interior emotional experience, which is well suited for a book, but more difficult to depict on screen. In addition to the book itself, we also had the intense, romantic, and visual experience of *Twilight*, and we had to sort of top both memories."

> "THE CHALLENGE FOR *New Moon* WAS, HOW DO WE GET ACROSS THE SENSE OF ABANDONMENT AND HEARTBREAK?"

A New Moon Rises

*Kristen Stewart
as Bella Swan.*

In NEW MOON, Bella Swan's eighteenth birthday is celebrated with a party at the home of Dr. Carlisle Cullen and his family of vampires. For Bella, it is more than a birthday party, it's a joyous acceptance into this brave new world, a beautiful chapter in her unfolding love story. But it only takes a paper cut and a pinprick of blood on her finger to awaken the primal bloodlust of the assembled vampires.

Edward later meets Bella at the house she shares with Charlie, her father. They take a walk in the woods, and he tells her the Cullen clan has decided to move away from Forks. It's time—how long could they stay in this little town, never aging, their secret vampire lives always at risk of exposure? "Don't do anything reckless or stupid," he orders her in the novel, telling her to look after her father. "…I promise that this will be the last time you'll see me. I won't come back. I won't put you through anything like this again. You can go on with your life without any more interference from me. It will be as if I'd never existed. . . . You're human—your memory is no more than a sieve. Time heals all wounds for your kind."[4]

And then, with a "goodbye, Bella," a press of his lips upon her forehead, and a passing breeze, he is gone.

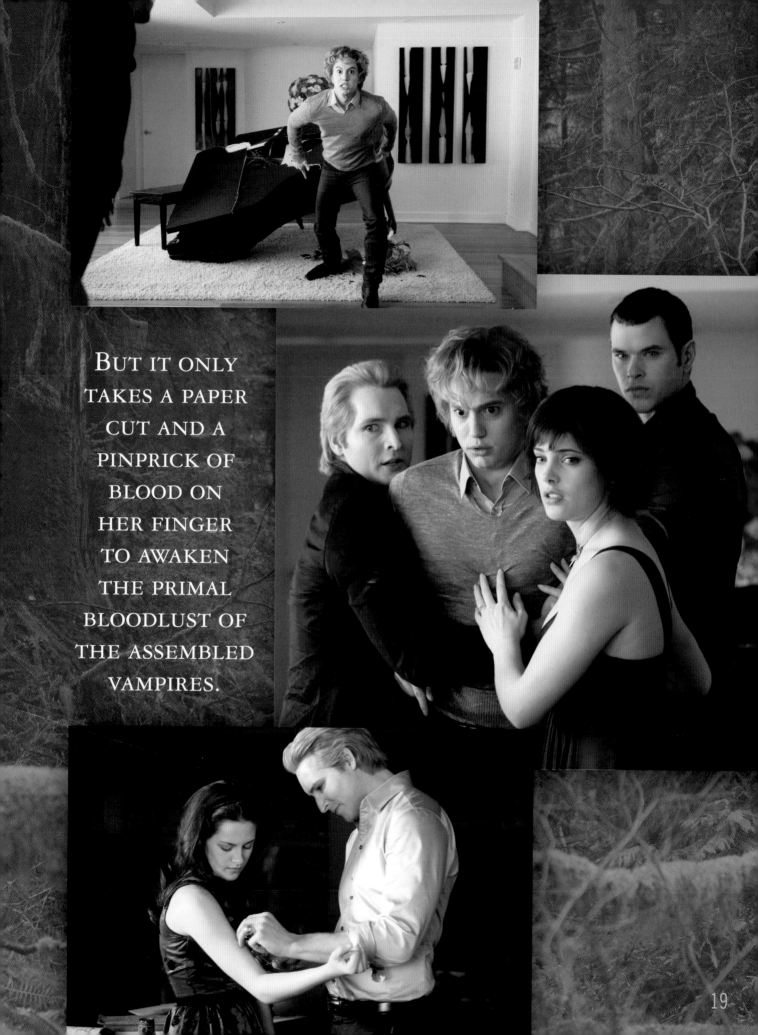

BUT IT ONLY
TAKES A PAPER
CUT AND A
PINPRICK OF
BLOOD ON
HER FINGER
TO AWAKEN
THE PRIMAL
BLOODLUST OF
THE ASSEMBLED
VAMPIRES.

19

Director of development Gillian Bohrer was a key part of the team involved in the creative end of moviemaking at Summit (from hiring the screenwriter and overseeing the screenplay to hiring a director and cast). She recalled the day when she got an eye-opening look at both the Stephenie Meyer phenomenon and an insight into the spirit of NEW MOON. In the fall of 2007, not long after Summit had bought the rights to TWILIGHT, Bohrer and Hardwicke went to a bookstore in Pasadena, California, to see Meyer. The author was on a book tour for ECLIPSE, her third novel in the series.

"Stephenie spoke to 1,400 fans," Bohrer recalled. "Only a few hundred could fit inside, the rest were wrapped around the bookstore. This was before [THE TWILIGHT SAGA] took over and became popular culture and the mainstream media. That day, when we sat down with Stephenie, she made the comment that most girls have only been in love once, if ever, and they believe there is one person in the universe for them. The idea that there is more than one

"I was filming the breakup scene with Bella, this big, traumatic scene, and there was like, literally, a plague of mosquitoes. I'd never seen so many mosquitoes in my entire life—and giant ones, as well. I could just tell when a mosquito was on the end of my nose and not be able to do anything about it. And they did not stop landing on us all night. So, it was not my favorite scene to film, but it was funny."

—ROBERT PATTINSON, ACTOR

person you can love, and more than one kind of love, is hard to fathom. NEW MOON is about that, about that first heartbreak and the healing process."

New Moon, the movie, was also about new beginnings—other than the producers and *Twilight* screenwriter Melissa Rosenberg, a new team of production principals was assembled. In a brief but tumultuous post-*Twilight* limbo period, the question of whether Hardwicke would direct the next movie was another hot topic among fans who had been dubbed "Twilighters." By early December, the official word was Hardwicke would not direct the next installment. One of the reported sticking points was the director's desire to spend more time on the screenplay. But time, from the studio's

perspective, was a luxury it couldn't afford. "Catherine had been at it 24/7 to get the film into the theaters and then all the publicity that followed the release," Godfrey noted, "and it was clear to us and the studio that we wanted to have *New Moon* for the following November 20. That was the date. The fans were desperate for *New Moon*."

"Development is about figuring out how to put a movie together," Bohrer added. "From a filmmaker's point of view, you need to know you have the raw material, and Catherine gave us an amazing foundation. We have an amazing cast, which Catherine put together. She was a vital part of getting this going."

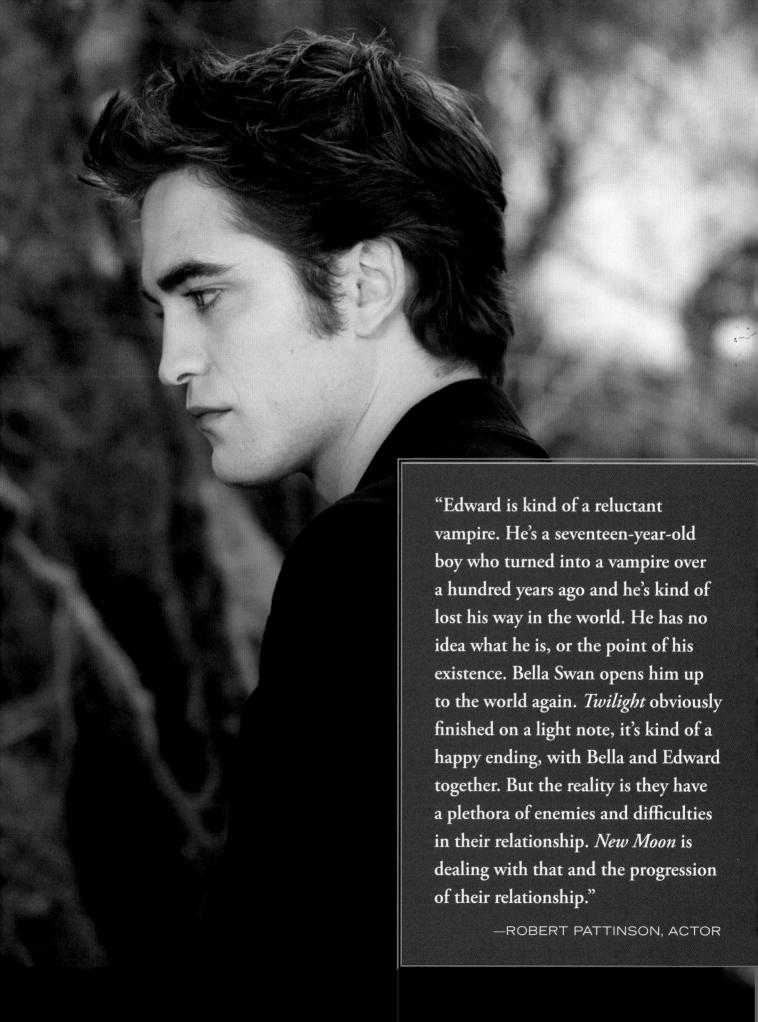

"Edward is kind of a reluctant vampire. He's a seventeen-year-old boy who turned into a vampire over a hundred years ago and he's kind of lost his way in the world. He has no idea what he is, or the point of his existence. Bella Swan opens him up to the world again. *Twilight* obviously finished on a light note, it's kind of a happy ending, with Bella and Edward together. But the reality is they have a plethora of enemies and difficulties in their relationship. *New Moon* is dealing with that and the progression of their relationship."

—ROBERT PATTINSON, ACTOR

The production demands of adapting NEW MOON were considerable. In the story, fresh prominence is given to Jacob Black, the young native Quileute who helps Bella start to ignore the emotional space left by Edward's absence, and who is also revealed as one of a pack of shape-shifting wolves. Bella is harassed by the vengeful vampires of TWILIGHT, Laurent and Victoria, and ultimately journeys to Italy to save Edward and face the Volturi, the ancient secret society of vampires that govern the shadowy vampire world. During their separation, Bella hears Edward's voice in her head whenever she is in danger, but in the movie Edward manifests as a visual presence the production labeled the "apparition."

All these plotlines and story points would require extensive computer graphics (CG) and digital visual effects work. As in the first film, the production would film in real locations, from Vancouver, Canada, to Italy and the Tuscan town of Montepulciano, the stand-in for the real Volterra, an ancient walled town that Meyer made the home of the sinister Volturi.

Although such locations could have been recreated on "greenscreen" soundstage sets (as in such stylized films as *Sin City* and *300*), the guiding light for *New Moon* was to make everything as real as possible. "One of the most lauded aspects of Stephenie's books is their realism," Godfrey noted. "You have vampires, but even then, they go to high school! So, to shoot *New Moon* like *300* wouldn't work for the audience who loves the books. We couldn't have done Italy on a stage, we had to go to a real location to have that square that is described in the novel. A stage set wouldn't have given us that same sense of reality, or given the audience the feeling of being taken to a

"THE TWILIGHT SAGA is a once-in-a-lifetime opportunity, and I'm really thankful to be part of it. On *Twilight*, we had no idea what we were making. We were like, 'Aw, this film is gonna be cool, hopefully some people like it.' The film's success has been really, really crazy and unexpected. I don't think any of us saw it coming, so it was a real crazy journey from when we finished *Twilight* to filming *New Moon*, which was kind of different. We came into it knowing what we were doing. And now, I guess we feel—at least I do—a little bit more pressure. We're like, wow—this is a phenomenon we're making. The fans are counting on us. They're like, 'You made *Twilight*, ...'"

place they'd never been before."

Given the complex nature of the production, its character-based drama and effects-filled spectacle, Summit's search for a director led to writer/director Chris Weitz, whose films range from the character-based comedy drama *About a Boy* (2002) to the fantasy spectacle *The Golden Compass* (2007), two films for which he did double duty as the screenwriter and director.

"On a movie of this scope, you want someone who understands action and stunts and special effects, but that is secondary to someone who understands emotion and story," Gillian Bohrer explained. "Chris has made emotional movies, and he also knows, on a technical level, how to work with effects, because he made *The Golden Compass* . . . Chris is a very focused, decisive, calm person who stepped into something with very little time. I never once heard him raise his voice. With everything being thrown at him, he just took it all in and figured it out."

"Erik Feig and I both knew Chris Weitz and had a comfort level with him," added Wyck Godfrey. "He's a writer and a director who understands character and has adapted literature, so remaining faithful to a book is just part of his genetic makeup. Secondly, he could handle the size of this movie and its visual effects demands, like he had done in *The Golden Compass*."

In addition to Weitz, production department heads would include production designer David Brisbin and art director Catherine Ircha, who had first worked together on the 2008 film *The Day the Earth Stood Still*. The recent work of director of photography Javier Aguirresarobe included another adaptation of a literary work, Cormac McCarthy's *The Road*. Weitz also

"HE'S A WRITER AND A DIRECTOR WHO UNDERSTANDS CHARACTER AND HAS ADAPTED LITERATURE, SO REMAINING FAITHFUL TO A BOOK IS JUST PART OF HIS GENETIC MAKEUP."

brought aboard as editor Peter Lambert, who had largely worked on independent films in Britain.

Helping the actors realize their characters were costume designer Tish Monaghan, key makeup artist Norma Hill-Patton, and key hairstylist Thom McIntyre.

Overseeing the visual effects challenge of creating shape-shifting werewolves, vampire effects, and other bits of movie magic fell to visual effects supervisor and producer Susan MacLeod, who had worked with Weitz as visual effects producer on *The Golden Compass*. MacLeod enlisted Tippett Studio, a storied visual effects and creature shop, to conjure computer-generated wolves, while Prime Focus of Vancouver handled the vampires and so-called "invisible" effects.

"The context of *New Moon* is different from *Twilight*, which is a more intimately shot movie. The scope and scale is much greater, and Chris [Weitz] wanted a movie in the style of *Barry Lyndon* or *Doctor Zhivago*. He felt that because Edward leaves, and we enter Jacob's world, he didn't want the cold, blue cast over the look of the movie [as seen in *Twilight*]. The coldness of Edward is replaced by the warmth of Jacob in this movie. What we latched on to was the despair of Bella having been left by Edward, that emotional void, and her being reborn through her relationship with Jacob, which, in some sense, brings her back to humanity."

—WYCK GODFREY, PRODUCER

As with the first film, Stephenie Meyer would be involved throughout the creative process, her mythic vision influencing everything from the screenplay to the postproduction visual effects work.

At the outset, the operative words were "aggressive schedule." To make the planned November 20, 2009, release date, Wyck Godfrey recalled, shooting began in Vancouver on March 23, 2009, and wrapped on May 21, and then it was off to shoot exterior locations in Italy from May 25 to May 30. When it was announced in early December of 2008 that

Hardwicke would not direct the sequel, Summit president Erik Feig was quoted as saying, "We are able to pursue an aggressive timeframe as we have the luxury of only adapting the novels into screenplays as opposed to having to create a storyline from scratch."[5]

Even as *Twilight* moved out of principal photography and into postproduction, the making of *The Twilight Saga: New Moon* had begun with screenwriter Melissa Rosenberg's fingers on the keyboard of her computer. Before *Twilight* had even opened, she turned in a first draft. Rosenberg's marathon schedule stretched from June through October of 2008, a period when her work-week was spent as an executive producer and head writer for the Showtime television series *Dexter*, and her weekends were reserved for *New Moon*.

"I would sit down at ten o'clock in the morning and work on *New Moon* through lunch until six o'clock in the evening," Rosenberg recalled. "I work in my house, looking out at trees, with my dog nearby and my husband bringing me snacks. I'd just pound it out; it got very intense. But I started with a detailed, twenty-five-page, single-spaced outline, which was really the hard part. The outline is where you're deconstructing the book and each character."

The creative dynamics had changed from when Rosenberg wrote the *Twilight* screenplay. Not only had the series grown in popularity, but now Meyer's characters had faces attached with actors breathing life into them. "On *Twilight* I tried to keep the fan base out of my head, but I couldn't avoid it by the time of *New Moon*," Rosenberg recalled. "But what fans love is the books, so if you take them on the same journey as the book, then you succeed. Now, with a

"IN THIS SERIES, THE HORROR ELEMENTS ARE THE BLOOD-RED ICING ON THE CAKE."

franchise, it's similar to writing for a television series. *Twilight* was like the pilot, it set the tone and was a discovery for everybody. But now you know the actors, the language, tone, and action."

Although every adaptation is based on existing material, Rosenberg happily notes she is the beneficiary of an embarrassment of riches when it comes to Meyer's work. "A lot of people who adapt books for the movies have less material to use. Stephenie Meyer has created such a rich mythology. But you can't translate a book directly to the screen. You have to pare it down to the essential tone and moments that convey the characters and their emotional journey. That's where you live and breathe. What's great is Stephenie has written these complex emotional arcs for her characters. And, in this series, the horror elements are the blood-red icing on the cake. It's fun to write all these dark and fantastical things, but what grounds them is the emotional state of the characters, that they are authentic."

Rosenberg kept in constant contact with Meyer while writing *New Moon*. She admits they were both initially wary—Meyer protective of her "baby," Rosenberg of her own creative process—but they quickly found common

"There are a million things to do on a movie, but, for me, the most important thing to start with, the essential starting point, is the script."

—GILLIAN BOHRER, SUMMIT ENTERTAINMENT, DIRECTOR OF DEVELOPMENT

*Bella (Kristen Stewart)
dreams of herself as an
old woman.*

creative ground and formed a close collaboration. "Stephenie has the whole mythology mapped out in her head," Rosenberg noted. "We would e-mail back and forth, regarding backstory questions and details."

One of the few scenes translated almost directly from novel to screenplay was Bella's opening dream sequence in which she sees Edward, "lovely and forever seventeen," as Meyer wrote, and herself as an old woman.[6] Translating that into screenplay terms was a matter of "just paring down," according to Rosenberg. But the screenwriter had to interpret the book for a visual medium, which was why she decided to take Edward's voice in Bella's head and make it visual.

The introduction of the "apparition" would become an emotional and visual underpinning for one of the major story points. In the novel, Edward's warning voice echoes in Bella's head during a night in the town of Port Angeles, when she walks past four young men (recalling another Port Angeles visit in TWILIGHT when four men threatened her). For the screenplay, Rosenberg gave those four men some motorcycles.

"This was the first moment that the apparition of Edward the protector comes forward and, for cinematic reasons, it needed to be a significant moment; it was not enough for her to just walk up to these guys, we wanted Bella to do something dangerous," Rosenberg explained. "I added the motorcycles, because she does this reckless thing and rides on one of the motorcycles, but motorcycles will also become an important part of her relationship with Jacob. It works really well because the motorcycles from Port Angeles stay in her head, as that was the situation that pushed Edward to appear. It's a visual touchstone."

Throughout, Rosenberg worked closely with the Summit creative team, including president of production Erik Feig and director

*During a night in Port Angeles,
Bella decides to be reckless.*

> "People always say Edward disappears [for most of NEW MOON], but he's very much a presence in Bella's thoughts. I chose to take that a step further and have him physically appear in her mind's eye."
>
> —MELISSA ROSENBERG, SCREENWRITER

of development Gillian Bohrer, as well as producers Karen Rosenfelt and Wyck Godfrey. Rosenberg, whose four movie screenplays (including the upcoming *The Twilight Saga: Eclipse*) were all produced at Summit, noted hers was rare good fortune for a screenwriter in Hollywood. "Summit makes what they develop," Rosenberg declared. "I have writer friends and it sounds like a nightmare at the bigger studios, where they develop things endlessly and keep hiring writers. They'll hire a writer to write the male lead or the woman's role, or hire someone to do a comedy pass. As a writer I can do all that—I write comedy, I write drama, that's what telling a story is. I think the more writers you have, the more watered down the [narrative] voice gets. That's why so much good work is going on in television, because screenwriters are the kings and queens of television, the show runners and writers are telling the story.

"For me, the screenwriter is like an architect and the screenplay is like an architectural plan," Rosenberg concluded. "You design every inch and foot, the feel and the rooms, and then you hire the designers and construction people who build the house. As any director will say,

you don't have a movie without a script. The old adage is you can make a bad movie from a good script, but you can't make a good movie from a bad script. It starts with me, then it's the director, the production designer, director of photography—everyone contributes to the tone."

After only a couple of drafts, Rosenberg's *New Moon* script was accepted toward the end of 2008. By January, the production race was on.

Chris Weitz ushered in 2009 by reading NEW MOON, and then he was off on a whirlwind. "I hadn't actually read the TWILIGHT books, so, over the New Year's vacation, I sat down and read the book in the way the readership usually experiences it—in one gulp. I read it over a day and a half and then I was off to Vancouver with my family. It was a rush, but in a good way. I had about eight weeks of prep, which would be normal for a film of just human beings talking. But for a film of this degree of complexity, with visual effects and specific locations, that was pushing it. But we managed somehow. There was something like 450 visual effects, which is less than on my previous film, *The Golden*

"Since *Twilight*, Jacob has changed physically, but he's transformed emotionally, too. So, I had to study the book and prepare myself mentally for his emotional state, as well as the physical. Jacob has been waiting for this moment when he finds out that Edward has left Bella. He's like, 'Sweet—it's my turn! ' [laughs]"

—TAYLOR LAUTNER, ACTOR

31

Compass, but was still a lot to organize."

Weitz noted that although his team had to be acceptable to the studio, he had freedom to follow his preferences. "Javier Aguirresarobe's cinematography is so beautiful, and he's also an extraordinary spirit, a good person to have on set, where the atmosphere is really important. And David Brisbin was so dedicated to making the film look right."

One of the major preproduction questions that was quickly answered was the casting of Jacob Black. Taylor Lautner had been one of the *Twilight* stars, but his slight build had raised the question of whether he could embody the Jacob of NEW MOON who suddenly becomes physically bigger as he attains the ability to become a werewolf.

"When I was filming *Twilight*, I knew where my character was going, so I knew I was going to have to change in many different ways," Lautner said. "So, the day after I finished filming, I began working out like crazy, and I put on thirty pounds. I was working out an hour in the morning and an hour and a half at night. My training schedule even got switched around a bit because I was actually overworking myself and had started losing weight. When I realized that, I toned things down, and started regaining my weight. It was a lot of hard work."

Producer Wyck Godfrey admitted the size issue was a concern, but also said that it would not have been good to start over with a new Jacob. "In the book Jacob has to transform, and the initial thought was if this actor can't visually represent the changed Jacob, then we're in trouble and we might have to recast. But, after *Twilight* opened, Taylor came in and said, 'See

what I've been doing?' At his age the body has a capacity to grow if you put effort into it, and, to credit Taylor's work ethic, he really did transform himself."

The Twilight Saga: New Moon, like every film, had to conjure a sense of place, a believable and cohesive world. To accomplish that, creative decisions ranged from the use of light and cameras to the color palette. The guiding principle, as noted earlier, was realism. "What is reality in a story about vampires and werewolves?" production designer David Brisbin rhetorically asked. "Chris really grounded us in reality, but he was also the one who pointed out [when something] needed to be magically real. Then it was all a matter of the options it takes to get there. If something requires a greenscreen, great! If it requires a stage set, great! If a location serves, that's fine. We didn't go into this feeling everything had to be *x* or *y*. We also had producers who were supportive of finding the optimum way to tell the story. . . *Twilight* was primarily a location movie; this was a hybrid of stage and location, with an even heavier CG exponent.

"I think 'conjuring' is very much a key word," explained Brisbin. "An enormous amount of what we do is how do you take time constraints, physical realities, and budget limits, and compress them with this magical space. A lot of it has to do with simple craft. We had a very experienced team working on this and we know a lot of tricks!"

"I love Taylor, he's my friend, and it's so weird to talk in an interview about your friends. But out of everybody in this movie, I think he's the one who stepped up in a way that's most impressive. What's funny is he's supposed to undergo a transformation in the movie, but it was cool to see that he did that in real life. He's growing into a really good guy, and he's really good in the movie. I'm so glad that I can look at someone every day [on the set] and believe every word that they say."

—KRISTEN STEWART,
ACTOR

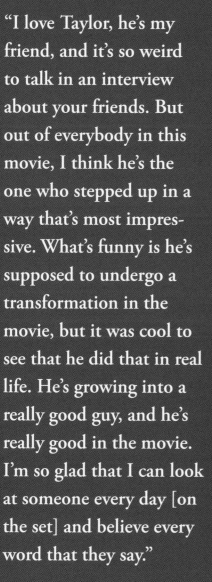

Chris Weitz directs Kristen Stewart and Taylor Lautner for a scene between Bella and Jacob.

33

Lost Moon

Kristen Stewart as Bella Swan.

Going back to Bella's world presented a challenge that every sequel must face—keeping things the same while making them different.

For *The Twilight Saga: New Moon*, director Chris Weitz envisioned a warm color palette. For inspiration he turned to the Pre-Raphaelite Brotherhood, an artistic community formed in 1848 by seven young painters with a dream.[7] "Chris Weitz is one of the most aesthetically astute directors I've ever worked with; he has a huge interest and a great awareness of the history of art," said David Brisbin. "He had very specific ideas as to the color world, the visual world, the atmosphere world. We moved the color palette away from where it stood on *Twilight*, because it's another phase in the story and it felt right to move into another color environment. For the look of the whole film, he pointed us to the Victorian painters, particularly the Pre-Raphaelites and the paintings of Dante Gabriel Rossetti and Edward Burne-Jones."

"The visual idea breaks with the first film in the saga," added director of photography Javier Aguirresarobe. "In this film we did without the blue tones that were prevalent in the previous film. Chris Weitz wanted to work with another kind of aesthetic, which led us to make a movie using golden tones. The change meant all departments would work in the same direction. We found our inspiration in Italian paintings, and our color palette—the golden tones, oranges, yellow-greens and neutral tones, grays and blacks—served as the basis for our collaborative work, from production design and wardrobe to, of course, photography. It is

a warmer-looking movie, and one closer to the romantic language."

The Pre-Raphaelites themselves represented not only a romantic look, but also a romantic view of life that fits well with the emotional terrain of Meyer's novels. "They were Victorian English painters who looked at Italian medi-

eval painting for inspiration regarding symbols, layout, and color," Weitz reflected. "Their work had the jewellike hues that you see in medieval painting, but they themselves were sentimental about looking backward. The Victorian period itself was romantic and sentimental, much in the way of Stephenie Meyer's novels. The color palette we used made the images crisper. We really wanted a wide range of colors and deep blacks, very saturated color, to go away from what is a more contemporary trend to desaturate, to do what would be, in painting terms, putting a glaze or varnish over things. In a sense, this is a very old-fashioned movie."

The approach included the use of specific colors at certain points in the story. For example, although Jacob's house is red, and there's a red coverlet on Bella's bed, the color doesn't dominate until a festival scene in the town square in Italy during the Volturi portion of the story. "Then the square becomes a flood of red," the director noted. "That's how conscious we were of every visual aspect."

The "old-fashioned" nature of the production included using film, not digital, cameras. Javier Aguirresarobe's arsenal included two main Panavision cameras, a high-speed Arri 435 camera capable of shooting at 150 frames per second, a Steadicam camera operated by David Crone (whom Weitz described as "one of the best Steadicam operators in the world"),

and VistaVision cameras for visual effects shots. As with the use of specific colors, the different cameras and shooting setups would serve the story points.

"I decided early on that I wanted the camera to move in different ways according to the relationship it was dealing with," Weitz explained. "So, when Bella is with Edward the camera moves on a dolly and on rails, it's always moving in a very straight line, the axis is very x-y-z, very rigid, because their relationship is about restraints. When Bella is with Jacob, we used a Steadicam, which is fluid and organic, and when she's with her schoolmates, it's more handheld, a sort of slangy visual language for the camera. Also, Javier is a big fan of long lenses, meaning beautiful shots portraying people and

Director Chris Weitz (left) with director of photography Javier Aguirresarobe.

"I remember, as if it were yesterday, the fantastic screenings of Technicolor films in my town, Éibar [Spain], images of movies about pirates and adventure stories that fascinated me. The first chance I got, I traveled to Madrid, and when I was old enough I studied at the Official Film School. For me there have been directors of photography that have been, and continue to be, my maestros. But there comes a time when it's more interesting to find your own way. Forget about this or that tendency, or even what might be in style. I like to immerse myself in the story and let that inspire me."

—JAVIER AGUIRRESAROBE, DIRECTOR OF PHOTOGRAPHY

*Camera operator David Crone
and director Chris Weitz.*

"But I have to come back to the fan issue," added Brisbin. "I've been a production designer for more than twenty years and this is the first time I've seen a fan base that is vocal and engaged in the idea that the movie is getting made. That was a new thing for me, it was very interesting and heartwarming. It was almost like working onstage—we could feel the audience was right there, in a way I'd never felt before. And it was a pleasure."

In addition to the aesthetic vision, the triumvirate of director, production designer, and director of photography were also concerned with matching the now iconic Portland locations. Another guiding design principle was to follow the vision and specific visual cues from the books. "When I was reading the book and screenplay I had some reservations [about the visual cues in the text]," Brisbin noted. "But, I have to admit, it became a valuable platform for

softer backgrounds, conveying the entirety of the space so everything is right in front of you."

The color palette, lighting, and camera work were designed to deliver an emotional impact. "One of the things we wanted to pull off for the fans was to keep our eye on the emotional ball of the story between Edward and Jacob and Bella," Brisbin noted. "We wanted to get inside of their backstory and psychological process, all the groundwork set up in the book, and also the groundwork done by the fans who get into the story and care about the story. We wanted to leverage all of that into a very tight psychological environment. Chris was quite diligent about keeping that as the guiding light in front of us.

> "IT WAS ALMOST
> LIKE WORKING
> ONSTAGE—WE
> COULD FEEL
> THE AUDIENCE
> WAS RIGHT
> THERE, IN A
> WAY I'D NEVER
> FELT BEFORE.
> AND IT WAS A
> PLEASURE."

us to build on. The interesting thing that developed between those of us making this film and this enormous fan base that writes about what they're thinking was we slowly came to understand how intensely and closely they had read the books—it counted for them that a precise color was part of the thing. So it became a source of visual strength that stretched through the writing of Stephenie through the screenplay to our director to what was hopefully in a scene."

> "A FILM SET IS NOT GLAMOROUS AT ALL! IT'S FOURTEEN-HOUR DAYS, YOUR FEET HURT, IT GETS MUDDY—BUT PEOPLE IN PHYSICAL PRODUCTION WILL TELL YOU THEY DO IT BECAUSE THEY LOVE IT."

Andi Isaacs, an executive vice president at Summit and head of physical production for all the studio's films, has come a long way from humble beginnings on the set of *The Bonfire of the Vanities*, the infamous 1990 film based on the Tom Wolfe novel (and a cautionary tale for adapting a literary work). "I started out as a craft service girl, serving coffee, and what was funny was at the time I said, 'I can't work in this industry—these people are crazy!'" Isaacs laughed. "But it's always a perfect storm [when things go wrong]. I learned early. A film set is not glamorous at all! It's fourteen-hour days, your feet hurt, it gets muddy—but people in physical production will tell you they do it because they love it."

"I wish filmmaking were as romantic as it might sound on the outside," Weitz agreed. "It's a lot of standing around in the rain and waiting—but, every now and then, you get wonderful moments of epiphany. But it's not like sitting down and playing a symphony. It's an accretion of thousands upon thousands of little decisions made over the course of months. It's every line reading, it's directing the animation of werewolves, it's the paint inside Jacob's house, it's about lavishing as much care as possible over every little detail."

Andi Isaacs's realm of physical production handles all the logistical, administrative, and financial concerns of making a film. When the creative side has developed a screenplay, the physical production department takes the script and does a cost breakdown. Once *The Twilight Saga: New Moon* went into production, producers Wyck Godfrey and Karen Rosenfelt represented Gillian Bohrer and the studio's creative concerns, while Andi Isaacs's key person in the field was line producer Bill Bannerman, whose staff addressed everything from how much things cost to making them happen—"the building process," as Bannerman put it. Essentially, he and his staff were intimately involved in the "thousands upon thousands of little decisions" that went into serving the needs of principal photography.

Among the first thousand decisions was where to shoot the film, and how to match locations from the first film. Even though the production team had loved shooting in Portland, ultimately it became more practical to stage principal photography in Vancouver, which over the years has built up the elaborate infrastructure vital to a movie production, from soundstage sets to a skilled technical and talent pool available for a production crew. In fact, Gillian Bohrer noted that Vancouver had been scouted as a potential setting for *Twilight*—and it was only because the U.S. dollar had, at that time, dropped below the Canadian dollar

There's a feeling on a movie set when you realize you're involved in something special. This is a subtle vampire movie, there isn't a lot of fangs and blood spurting. It's a fun world to create, a beautiful world, a romantic world. We all wanted to make a movie we could be proud of, not just a success on a monetary level, but something that will be remembered."

—ANDI ISAACS, SUMMIT ENTERTAINMENT, HEAD OF PHYSICAL PRODUCTION

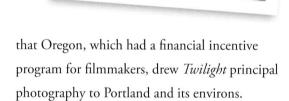

that Oregon, which had a financial incentive program for filmmakers, drew *Twilight* principal photography to Portland and its environs.

"It made a significant difference in dollars to shoot in Vancouver, it allowed us to get more production value," Isaacs explained. "It was not only a lot more film friendly, it was chosen because it was beautiful, with forests and gray weather. At the same time, we weren't going to cheat for the locations [seen in] *Twilight*. For example, we built a set of Bella's house, we re-created the home from the first film, because we knew our fans would notice if we shot *New Moon* with a different house—it's the 'movie magic' thing. But there were so many benefits to going to Vancouver that to re-create a few locations from *Twilight* was well worth it."

Other *Twilight* locations that had to be replicated included the Cullen house, Forks High School, and even the magical meadow where Bella first saw Edward glittering in the sunlight. There were also new locations that had to be found, such as Jacob's house. In addition to the use of soundstage facilities, notably for a grand set of the great marble hall of the Volturi, the location needs were served by Vancouver location manager Abraham Fraser, whose own career started as a production assistant on the pilot for *The X-Files* television series, which originally filmed in Vancouver.

With a considerably shortened prep time before principal photography began in late March, Fraser and his crew started the week of December 20 and were in high gear after the holidays. In early January, Fraser, Weitz, and Brisbin scouted the Portland area locations that had to be matched in Vancouver. But there were bitter weather conditions awaiting Fraser when he returned from Portland. "We had solid snow that changed into thick fog, which made our first month of scouting very difficult," Fraser recalled. "Some locations, like a road I wanted for the Forks Highway, I couldn't present because there was the fear that it could still be under snow. Because of our shooting schedule, I was not convinced the snow would be gone when we were ready to shoot there. We ended up choosing a different road, south and away from the mountains at a lower elevation which didn't have snow."

Despite the disappointment of the lost Forks Highway, other dream locations presented themselves as the snow melted or was plowed, such as the magical meadow, which becomes a place of terror for Bella in NEW MOON. "I knew of a perfect location for the meadow and although there was still a little snow on the ground, it was enough to see what the setting would be," Fraser said. "The director loved it immediately."

The location department finished its scouting by the end of February, but was involved throughout filming. They prepped locations for shooting by making sure local police departments and residents were alerted that a film crew and cameras and equipment trucks would be in their neighborhood, and that all necessary permissions and contracts had been secured.

Movie magic was needed for the Forks High School exterior and cafeteria. For the

From top: Weitz with Stewart on set; Christian Serratos as Angela and Justin Chon as Eric; Edward and Bella in class; the Forks High School cafeteria set.

"Any kind of mistake can be very costly. If you don't have the right paperwork in place, or the contract is not solid and you have no place to shoot the next day, you're in big trouble."

—ABRAHAM FRASER,
LOCATION MANAGER

exterior, a parking lot was found, but it required re-creation of the school steps. A greenscreen backing was used so later they could add the image of the original high school exterior. The cafeteria, while not a perfect match, was close enough. "We want to feel as though we're in the right school, but we weren't able to see the entire room because it wasn't the same cafeteria," Fraser noted. "But now that we have it, we have a place to shoot for the next two movies."

Alice (Ashley Greene) insists on giving Bella a birthday party.

The Cullen house was one of the major "match" assignments, particularly as the Portland area location from *Twilight*—the so-called "Nike house"—was unique in its design. The decision was made to find a house in the Vancouver area with an interior that emulated the high ceilings, glass walls, and forest surroundings of the first location. "The Cullen house used for *Twilight* was a very specific house, and the only way out of that puzzle for us was to put portions of the story in *New Moon* in other parts of the house," Brisbin explained.

"We scouted for other locations for the Cullen house, but I always knew of a house that would be a slam dunk," Fraser said. "It was surrounded by trees, there were a lot of windows, large open floor space, clean lines—

it was a good match."

"It was compatible enough with the house in Portland, and I hope the fans will be able to feel it is of a piece," Brisbin added.

One of the first glimpses of *The Twilight Saga: New Moon* that the fans got to see was Bella's birthday party scene, shots of which appeared in the first teaser trailer for the film. Of course, this scene was filmed in the new location. "It had these enormously tall ceilings, and this lovely stairway that allowed you to see the world as you sort of descended into it," elaborated Brisbin. "The space had to be something unusual because the birthday party scene there represents an important step in Bella's life. She is basically taken into the magic party of her life, the party that everyone would dream of at that age."

Weitz echoed Brisbin's emphasis on a magical mood, one set in the warm, romantic range of the production's color palette. "For Bella's birthday party, we wanted to capture that fantasy aspect—what if you had these wealthy, wonderful, sophisticated friends who gave you the most beautiful birthday party imaginable? The aim was to feel quite warm and candlelit, as opposed to electric and tungsten lights."

"I wanted an especially 'hot' environment for this sequence, we avoided the blue tones [of the first film]," Javier Aguirresarobe explained.

"I made use of the candles all over the place. We wanted to give the feeling that this is a normal family. The light gave an intimate touch, but also recalled the time when Edward and Bella were first attracted to each other and in love. The light was filtered in hot tones, its texture was smooth and it had a low intensity. It's an important sequence. Edward relates the history of the Volturi to Bella, she becomes wounded in the hand, and Edward faces off against Jasper."

"FOR BELLA'S BIRTHDAY PARTY, WE WANTED TO CAPTURE THAT FANTASY ASPECT—WHAT IF YOU HAD THESE WEALTHY, WONDERFUL, SOPHISTICATED FRIENDS WHO GAVE YOU THE MOST BEAUTIFUL BIRTHDAY PARTY IMAGINABLE?"

"The birthday scene at the Cullen house is like the ideal birthday party. The house is beautifully decorated and everyone is very happy. Edward is looking at Bella and thinking that she can become part of his family and his life—that maybe this can work out the way he wants it to."

—ROBERT PATTINSON, ACTOR

Jasper (Jackson Rathbone) can't control himself when he smells Bella's blood.

"Things go wrong in a rather frightening way, there's this sudden outburst of violence," the director added. "We wanted to have people thrown through the air and have heft and weight to them, not have it feel like they're on wires."

The stunt work was complicated because they were in a real house and couldn't drill holes for their wire rigs. Stunt coordinator J.J. Makaro explained that he and his team had to carefully plan the brief outburst of violence that ends the party and do it quickly. The director first had to film his part of the sequence with the actors and first unit, and they would go in the next day and stage and execute the action. "But we were lucky, because the house had like a fifteen-foot roof above and we could attach our truss work up there, although that in itself was a big piece of machinery and we had to keep it out of the shots," Makaro explained.

STUNT COORDINATOR J.J. MAKARO EXPLAINED THAT HE AND HIS TEAM HAD TO CAREFULLY PLAN THE BRIEF OUTBURST OF VIOLENCE THAT ENDS THE PARTY AND DO IT QUICKLY.

Scouting for the house Bella shares with her father was only a "soft search," as Abraham Fraser put it. "We didn't waste a lot of time searching because, even in Oregon, that was a rare home. That house is about a hundred years old, and of a rare design for that period—even the owners hadn't seen another like it. Finding that house was going to be difficult, so we wanted to cheat it to look like the real home. It evolved rather quickly that we would have to find an empty lot to build [a re-creation]. We used a rural

"MAYBE IF SOMEONE TOOK A MAGNIFYING GLASS THEY COULD FIND THE AREAS WHERE WE CHEATED, BUT WE GOT AS CLOSE AS WE COULD COME."

and underused city park. This empty land had the right geographic setting, with a tree line and road coming up. The production built a shell of the home, all four sides, and cut down and planted some trees in front to match. That set will stay there until we're completed with the franchise."

Once a site for Bella and Charlie's house had been found, the design and construction departments had to replicate the house itself. Brisbin characterized the challenge as an exception to the usual process by which a set is dreamed up and built from

This New Moon *set re-created the house used for Bella and Charlie's home in* Twilight.

scratch. "We had to measure the house in Portland and build the exterior of the house on the Vancouver location, while the interior, upstairs and downstairs, was built on a stage in Vancouver. Maybe if someone took a magnifying glass they could find the areas where we cheated, but we got as close as we could come. We studied the locations from the first film and, most important, the *Twilight* footage to see what, at the end of the day, the camera sees. If you look at the way it's cut in the first film, it feels like Bella's bedroom is in the front of the house—in fact, it's not, it's on the right-hand side of the house [facing the front]."

While it was doable to draw up architectural specifications to duplicate the house, inside and out, the original Oregon house had been

repainted since *Twilight*, making for a different look from what had been captured on film. "A lot of the aging and texture was removed when the house was painted," art director Catherine Ircha noted. "We had references for that house before, during, and after it was shot, but this massive amount of imagery didn't necessarily show the beautiful aging and texturing we had seen on *Twilight*. So where was the aging reference to come from?"

The reference came, as David Brisbin noted, from the first movie itself, beginning with stills pulled from low-resolution DVDs. "We couldn't see a lot of detail on the low-resolution DVDs, so I got the high-definition Blu-ray disc of *Twilight* the instant it came out," Ircha said. "That was completely eye-opening! Until I saw

that Blu-ray, there were a lot of things that I had no idea existed. It was amazing.

"We talked about the textures in Bella's bedroom, but when you watched it in high-def it was extreme, the walls were massively textured. They had a kind of stucco finish, a bumpy texture that stuck out a quarter of an inch in places. And you could see the shadow—at lower-res you couldn't see that. There was also one quick shot of the bedroom floor in *Twilight*, but we decided to match it because it was right there on screen, you couldn't deny it. We had time after seeing the Blu-ray, nothing in production was past the point where we couldn't alter things."

Ircha remembered that when there were only poor quality DVD still pulls to reference Bella's old pickup truck, she used TWILIGHT: THE COMPLETE ILLUSTRATED MOVIE COMPANION, the 2008 making-of book, as a resource. "That book was the best reference for Bella's truck, there were these incredibly beautiful shots of the truck.

"David and I are perfectionists, we really cared about the minutiae, we cared about every little thing," Ircha added.

One special challenge for the production team was how to convey Bella's depression once Edward departs. In Meyer's novel, Bella describes the separation as an emotional tidal wave that washes over and pulls her under. From there, the novel has blank pages, with only months printed upon them: October... November... December... January.

That passage of time would be represented in the film as a visual effects shot, with Kristen Stewart sitting in a chair in Bella's bedroom as the camera circled around her and provided a view of the changing seasons outside her window. The effect required a slight adjustment on what had been an otherwise a meticulous re-creation of Bella's home. "To get that shot we needed to relate Bella to the main window of her bedroom," Brisbin explained, "but the window in the original bedroom really wasn't sufficient to do that. So we created a bit more space [for a bay window] because of the story relationship to the forest outside her house."

The effect was one of the estimated 300 visual effects shots helmed by Prime Focus. Formerly called Frantic Films, the company has garnered both Emmy and Academy Award nominations for its work. To Prime Focus visual effects supervisor Eric Pascarelli and overall effects head Susan MacLeod, the scene was a "transition shot," an elegant way to capture Bella's emotional state and the passage of time. "We called this shot 'time passing,'" Pascarelli said. "The camera is supposed to orbit her three times, three hundred sixty degrees, and every time we pass the bay window another month has passed."

It required matching up two different camera shots—the one focused on the actress in Bella's bedroom soundstage set, the other shooting the view outside the window as seen from the house built on location. The first choice was to shoot "motion control," a computer programmable and repeatable system by which separately shot elements can be filmed with the same camera move. Then the separate elements are composited together to create a single seamless image. However, the bedroom set was too small to accommodate standard motion control equipment.

"Susan had a custom dolly track made and we had motion control camera operator Paul Maples and Craig Shumard of Pacific Motion Control in L.A. attach little encoders to the dolly on set," Pascarelli explained. "That recorded information could then be fed into the motion control system so the exact camera move could be recreated at the Bella location house. . . . The location house itself was a very friendly set, solid and capable of handling thousands of pounds [of equipment]. Bella's room is on the second floor, so we got our motion control camera up there to shoot from inside looking out. We removed the

"I think what's fantastic about Stephenie Meyer's series is she took these mythical creatures, vampires and werewolves, which everyone thinks they know about, and reinvented them. And Bella Swan is every girl, but relatable to women and men and all ages. The tug for Bella between Edward and Jacob is such a relatable experience."

—ERIK FEIG,
SUMMIT ENTERTAINMENT,
PRESIDENT OF PRODUCTION
AND ACQUISITIONS

Charlie (Billy Burke) worries about Bella.

51

window frame, so we could get the view outside, we had something like an eight-foot-tall by ten-foot-wide opening."

"We shot three different backgrounds [for the view out the window], one for fall, one for Thanksgiving, one for winter and Christmastime," MacLeod added. "In addition to replacing the greenscreen element on the soundstage bedroom set with the outdoor views, Prime Focus enhanced the changing of the seasons with computer-generated leaves for what we called 'Jacob's tree' [at one point in the story, Jacob climbs up it to see Bella], and CG falling snow."

"It was challenging for Kristen to go to those emotional places Bella goes to in the book," Wyck Godfrey observed. "The months where Edward leaves are just a void for Bella, and we came up with a very cool visual way to represent what was in the books."

Although film editing is usually classified as part of postproduction, shots were being assembled throughout principal photography. Film editor

Outtakes from a scene that may not make the final film cut: Bella has a nightmare of being in the forest, in a weird version of her bedroom. Edward and a wolf appear.

Peter Lambert recalled some good-natured eyebrows raised by the location manager and production designer as he started work six weeks before shooting began. His preproduction work included scanning in drawn storyboards to create computer-generated "previz" concepts, a commonly used previsualization technique by which the look of a scene, from blocking to camera angles, can be explored through low-resolution CG characters and environments. "A lot of previz was done for Edward's apparition, the manifestation that appears to Bella whenever she gets into danger," Lambert noted.

The editor's preproduction period was also spent working out "the language of the film" with the director. "One thing Chris and I discussed was the transitions that could tell the story in the most efficient way. For example, after Bella sees the werewolves, there was a sequence we cut of her running through the woods to her truck, driving off, arriving home, and running in to tell her father what she's seen. It was actually more effective to have her run out of the woods and cut immediately to, 'Dad, I saw them!' "

A real wolf was brought onto the set for the dream sequence.

53

An invention for the film was the birthday gift that Jacob gives to Bella. In the school parking lot, he arrives to hand her a dream catcher. Later in the film it hangs over Bella's bed. Production designer David Brisbin noted that while the dream catcher is not necessarily native to the Quileute, he felt director Chris Weitz wanted to rejigger the potential touristy connotation of the object for the sake of craft and a dramatic device.

"Chris has an enormous interest in the history of arts and crafts and particularly in 'outsider' works," said Brisbin. He relishes eclectic combinations and reinventions." The dream catcher stirs up emotions in all the major characters. "The bottom line," continued Brisbin, "is that the dream catcher within the story symbolizes exactly what the characters point to. Jacob says that it will catch bad dreams, Edward is irritated that his rival gives Bella an intimate gift, Charlie later expresses regret that it didn't keep on working."

Like all the other key props, this one was created through a process where the propmaster Ellen Freund found research and comissioned protoypes. Chris Weitz specified he did not want any feathers on it. The team also thought about how it would be carried and handled between Jacob and Bella, which determined scale and weight. The pouch it came in was a suggestion of Freund's.

"The prop was created in parts," said Ellen Freund. "The grapevine frame and web was woven by a woman in Wisconsin. It was chosen for its unusual and relatively complex design. The beading was added locally by Jenny McDonnell. Jenny also created the deerskin pouch the dream catcher was carried in. The silver wolf was cast by a local Vancouver artist."

Jacob gives Bella her birthday present.

The production team created three identical props and two back-ups that weren't as exact a match.

Lambert added that when editors generally talk about "cutting" a film, it means assembling a coherent sequence, not cutting out scenes. The variety of camera angles selected for any given scene helps the filmmakers convey the key narrative points or emotions they wish to convey.

"An example is the scene in which Edward breaks up with Bella," Lambert said. "The actors are shot from different angles—a wide shot, a two-shot, close-ups—with a number of different takes from all those angles. The particular angles chosen have an enormous impact on how an audience will read that moment. If you see an extreme wide shot, perhaps it means they're being watched. If you hear Edward's voice, but are looking at Bella's face, you're focusing on her reaction. So, I'm not 'cutting' things out, I'm making choices of which moments to show."

Every day, film editor Peter Lambert would go back and forth from his cutting-room facility to the particular location where he would watch dailies with director Chris Weitz and producer Wyck Godfrey. Lambert laughed that, having the luxury of a car and driver and to save time, he would work on editing the film during his daily commute. "The laptop system was set up by Kindra Marra, my amazing first assistant editor. I think this might have been the first major motion picture in which the biggest portion of the first assembly of the film was edited in the backseat of a car."

> "THE PARTICULAR ANGLES CHOSEN HAVE AN ENORMOUS IMPACT ON HOW AN AUDIENCE WILL READ THAT MOMENT."

Weitz directs Pattinson for the good-bye scene.

"As a sign that she's committed to Edward, she also wears clothes that are linked to him, color-wise."

Creating an updated look for Bella in *New Moon* involved balancing her recognizable qualities from *Twilight* with the need to show the character's progression. "We wanted to keep Bella rooted in the real world, an earth-tone color palette, and maintain the small-town quality of Forks," costume designer Tish Monaghan explained. "At the same time, Kristen wanted her character, who's a year older, to show a little more maturity. We did keep a few favorite bits from the first film, like her sneakers, a couple jackets, some of the jeans. But, as a sign that she's committed to Edward, she also wears clothes that are linked to him, color-wise. So, in their scenes together before Edward disappears, we made the conscious choice to steer her [wardrobe] to grays, purples, and blues."

With Edward's departure, Bella falls into despair. "When Edward disappears and Bella retreats into a depressive funk for months, we moved to darker, moodier, and, I would even say, unkempt, clothing for her," Tish Monaghan said. "The point is, she's so upset she doesn't pay as much attention to her appearance.

> "THE POINT IS, SHE'S SO UPSET SHE DOESN'T PAY AS MUCH ATTENTION TO HER APPEARANCE."

*Author Stephenie Meyer on set with
Kristen Stewart and Taylor Lautner.*

*The props on Bella's dresser include a
picture of Edward and her friends at
Forks High School.*

Bella goes to the movies with Jacob and Mike.

"THE INITIAL CHALLENGE FOR ME WAS MAINTAINING WHAT WAS SUCCESSFUL IN THE FIRST FILM, IN TERMS OF CREATING A REAL WORLD. . .I THOUGHT THE PREVIOUS DESIGNER DID A REALLY GOOD JOB OF STUDYING SMALL-TOWN LIFE, AND I WANTED TO CONTINUE THAT WITH BELLA'S WORLD, HER FATHER'S WORLD, THE WORLD OF BELLA'S FRIENDS IN FORKS."

—TISH MONAGHAN, COSTUME DESIGNER

Earthbound Sun

Taylor Lautner as Jacob Black.

"Well, there are lots of legends, some of them claiming to date back to the Flood—supposedly, the ancient Quileutes tied their canoes to the tops of the tallest trees on the mountain to survive like Noah and the ark. . . .

"Another legend claims that we descended from wolves—and that the wolves are our brothers still. It's against tribal law to kill them.

"Then there are the stories about the *cold ones*. . . .

"You see, the cold ones are the natural enemies of the wolf—well, not the wolf, really, but the wolves that turn into men, like our ancestors. You would call them werewolves."

—JACOB BLACK[8]

In TWILIGHT, during a walk along First Beach—a mile-long, crescent-shaped beach near La Push—Jacob explains to Bella that his great-grandfather knew the leader of a local group of "cold ones" who didn't hunt like others of their kind, who lived on the blood of animals instead of humans. Still, since it was in the nature of the cold ones to lust for human blood, Jacob's ancestor didn't want them near his people. So he made a truce with the leader of the vampire clan: the cold ones would stay off tribal lands, and the Quileute would not reveal their presence to the white man.

Bella compliments Jacob on his flair for storytelling, trying to as act as if it's just a scary story, even as Jacob asks her not to tell anyone what he has revealed.

Bella would be living the truth soon enough.

The whispered rumors of strange creatures stalking the forests around Forks become an eerie undercurrent in NEW MOON. While readers eventually know the real threat is from the bloodthirsty vampire Victoria of TWILIGHT, who has come back for Bella, the whispers also herald the emergence of the legendary werewolves, with Jacob among the supernatural wolf pack. As Melissa Rosenberg's screenplay puts it, there's "something in the woods."

Jacob and his friends on the Quileute reservation emerge as a major focus of Meyer's second novel, and the filmmakers dove into putting the Quileute world on the big screen. During the short preproduction period, a location scout visited Quileute country in Wash-

ington. "The location is incredibly beautiful," David Brisbin reflected. "You drive through this thick mountain forest and come down and you see this fantastic bay and rock pinnacles sticking up. The actual town hugs the coastline, backed up by these dramatic mountains.

"We did give some thought to whether Jacob's house would be in the community," said Brisbin. "But, for story reasons, we decided to poke around the edges of Quileute territory. We found some in-between spaces which were not physi-

cally on the reservation, but attached to it, where there were farmlike dwellings. That's where we settled on the paradigm of Jacob's house, the logic of Jacob's world, which is closer to the forest than the town itself.

"The driving force of Jacob's world was to exhibit all of Jacob's warmth and genuineness, but also this very intense relationship to the forest. In Chris's mind, Jacob's house was like a stepping stone into the forest world, where the reality of the werewolf story is hidden, so Chris wanted it to be separate

"JACOB'S HOUSE WAS LIKE A STEPPING STONE INTO THE FOREST WORLD."

enough that special things could happen there. And Emily's house, which is like a den club for the young men of the tribe, is even more separated from regular life, even deeper in the forest, and more connected to the magical life they are entering and getting to know."

Jacob's house presented a conundrum to the production designer, who was trying to follow the "visual cues" of Meyer's novels. "In the script [and the books] it's identified as a red house, and Bella even mentions it's like a red-colored barn," Brisbin recalled. "We found a location outside Vancouver that the director, the director of photography, and myself all felt was the perfect world. It was a barn where the motorcycles [that Bella and Jacob work on together] could be repaired, and it had this beautiful forest around the edges. We knew it

The exterior of the house where Sam Uley lives with his great love, Emily.

was the right place. But the place was green, it was a beautiful green world. I struggled with whether to follow the gift of the location, or the gift of Stephenie Meyer."

It was decided to follow both—after a Photoshop design proved the look would work, the location was secured for filming and painted red. "I had showed them the land, the space," location manager Fraser recalled, "and it was a green house with a fence wrapped around it. The owner was a goat herder, with a farm. We removed the fence, painted the barn red and aged it, added touches of native art, carvings and whatnot, with old trailers and boats dressing the set to imply it was near the water. David Brisbin recreated the whole layout to be more of Jacob's character."

Although the farm was in an isolated area, Twilighters still found it, providing Brisbin with

"The world of the Quileute is the world of nature. There is also an interior world, which is Emily's house, which is totally integrated in the forest. I always tried to use lighting which could be justified by the sources of natural light like the sun, whether it was direct or filtered by the clouds. The visual impression I wanted to express is that of a pleasant place, where warm green tones predominate. I tried a somewhat fantastic recreation of an environment expected to be very close to the wild."

—JAVIER AGUIRRESAROBE, DIRECTOR OF PHOTOGRAPHY

Javier didn't use a lot of smoke and fog effects, just the beauty of the locations. But it's all an illusion. We're creating the illusion of vampires, the illusion that Jacob can transform into a wolf. The challenge [for filmmakers] is to have audiences sit in a dark movie theater for two hours and be transported to another world, to go from disbelief to belief."

—NORMA HILL-PATTON, KEY MAKEUP

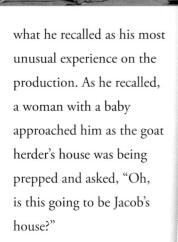

Kristen Stewart gets ready for a scene in front of Jacob's house.

what he recalled as his most unusual experience on the production. As he recalled, a woman with a baby approached him as the goat herder's house was being prepped and asked, "Oh, is this going to be Jacob's house?"

"That question was a shocker to me," Brisbin said. "Usually, people will ask, 'Are you shooting a movie?' She was many steps ahead. The studio had asked us to be as discreet as humanly possible about what we were doing, so things could be as much of a surprise as possible when the movie came out. So, I kind of hedged. She said, 'Yes, but I can see how you made it look old, and Jacob's house looks old.' There was no denying the truth! 'Yes, it's Jacob's house.'"

"THE STUDIO HAD ASKED US TO BE AS DISCREET AS HUMANLY POSSIBLE ABOUT WHAT WE WERE DOING, SO THINGS COULD BE AS MUCH OF A SURPRISE AS POSSIBLE WHEN THE MOVIE CAME OUT... [BUT] THERE WAS NO DENYING THE TRUTH! 'YES, IT'S JACOB'S HOUSE.'"

The production was shadowed by fans from Vancouver to Italy. With cell phone cameras and instant Internet access, in the twinkling of an eye, the latest from the production front was instantly streaming through the worldwide virtual network of fans. Although art director Catherine Ircha's main responsibility was making sure the director and production designer's vision came to fruition on the sets and locations, she took it upon herself to be a scholar of all four books and make sure the production maintained fan-friendly continuity. "When you're doing a movie, things go very quickly," she explained, "and a lot of people hadn't had a chance to read all of the books. I was also keeping an eye on the fan sites and blogs. My focus was really to include the vision of the book, and make the movie the fans wanted to see and stay true to it for them."

"When we were shooting, the fans were very respectful. When we asked them to be quiet during filming, they'd be quiet. When we said, 'Cut,' they'd start talking and screaming and clapping. Filming at the high school was a fun day. They built a little tunnel barrier to get actors in and out, but there were no problems. You just have to recognize the fans are what makes your movie successful, and we try to treat them with the utmost respect."

—ANDI ISAACS, SUMMIT ENTERTAINMENT, HEAD OF PHYSICAL PRODUCTION

Ircha's diligence paid off in an incident that played out against the backdrop of Jacob's house. "In NEW MOON there's no mention of the color of Jacob's car, but in ECLIPSE it says his car is red," Ircha recalled. "At the location set for Jacob's house they had put out a different car for set dressing, a blue Volkswagen Rabbit. When you're painting an old barn red, all the fans know it's Jacob's house even though the place was off the beaten track. It was a Saturday and all the fans were blogging. Within that weekend they had posted pictures online and people had started to write saying it's blue, [but] it's supposed to be red."

According to Ircha, it had just been an extra car—Jacob would have his red car in *New Moon*. "That detail is so easy to skip, it's just briefly mentioned, a book ahead," Ircha said. "Wyck caught the red car thing, too. But I did stress out and got no sleep over that weekend. Horrible!"

As screenwriter Melissa Rosenberg noted, motorcycles come into Bella's life a few times in the film, both as symbols of danger and of her journey. "The motorcycle stuff is basically the development of Bella and Jacob's friendship," said Taylor Lautner. "Bella brings over these bikes in the back of her pickup and it's like, 'Hey! I wanna start riding dirt bikes.' Jacob goes, 'Are you sure? Okay, then let's get to work.' So, there's this cool montage and as they're building these motorcycles they start becoming closer. By the end, when the bikes are finally ready to ride, they're having fun with each other. It's definitely a symbol for their whole relationship."

"Jacob [for Bella] is the attainable. He is the friend who will always be there for her. She is in such a deep depression when Edward leaves, and Jacob is her sun. He is the one who brings her out of this depression and keeps her alive."

—TAYLOR LAUTNER, ACTOR

In addition to motorcycles being the means by which Bella and Jacob bond, the motorcycle incident in Port Angeles makes Bella realize she can summon Edward's presence. "Bella comes to realize that any surge of adrenaline, for whatever reason, ignites not only a subjective image she has of Edward, like a memory, but she also gets to hear his voice and what she imagines he would be telling her in these moments of pure stupidity he's warned her about before he left," Kristen Stewart said. "So, she's willing to throw herself off cliffs [to go water diving] and get on motorcycles, which is not a Bella thing. Bella is not a risk taker, but she becomes addicted... She's just making it worse, she has a need to see him."

As Jacob helps Bella come out of her depression, her freshly blossoming spirit is shown in her costumes with brighter colors and springtime shirts with short sleeves—"happier" clothing, as the costume designer called it. Meanwhile, Jacob's wardrobe was designed to emphasize Lautner's physique. "We kept Jacob primarily in T-shirts, even tailoring the sleeves to augment his muscles," Monaghan noted. "We shortened his long-sleeve shirts, as if he was growing out of his clothes. We had him in boots to add to his height, and put Bella in flat shoes to emphasize the size difference between them.

"We kept Jacob in earth tones and greased up his jeans, because he spends a lot of time in his garage, where the unspoken attraction between Jacob and Bella develops as they work on the motorcycles. But I also wanted to show that Jacob's world is very different from Edward's world, and that Bella is caught between the two."

"Bella is using [Jacob], although never consciously, at least initially. When she discovers she's using him, it's a terrible thing because he is in love with her. But she's in a desperate state of mind over the loss of Edward and she's not particularly aware of other people's feelings. What also takes her by surprise is she realizes she's developing feelings for Jacob. He makes her feel a little more at peace, so she gravitates to him."

—MELISSA ROSENBERG, SCREENWRITER

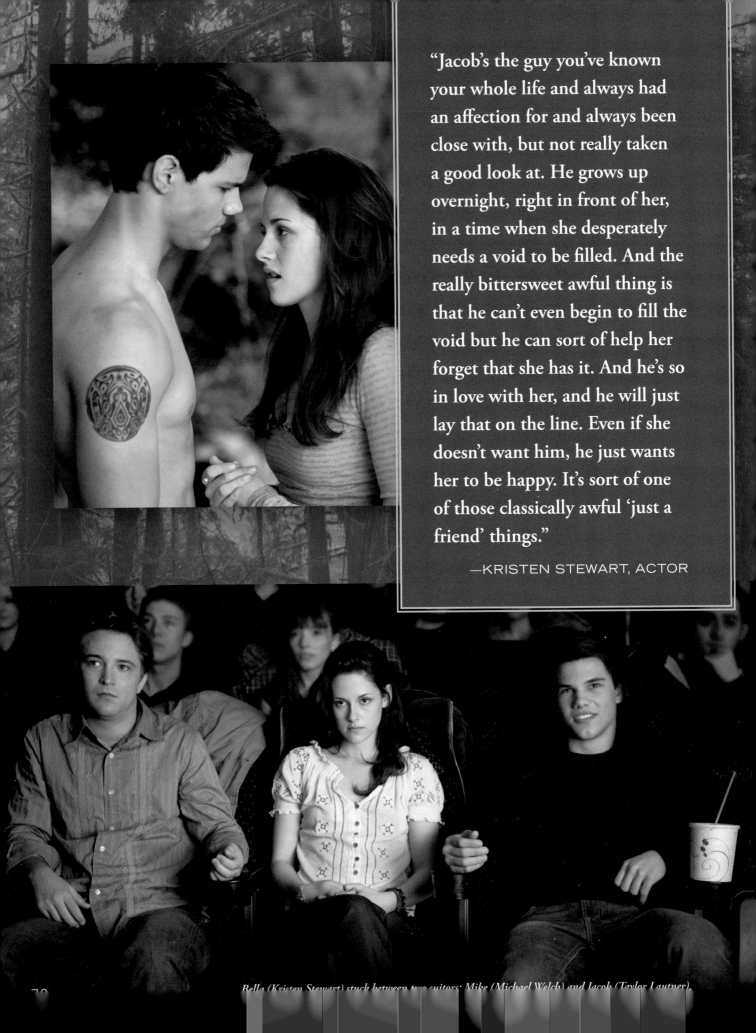

"Jacob's the guy you've known your whole life and always had an affection for and always been close with, but not really taken a good look at. He grows up overnight, right in front of her, in a time when she desperately needs a void to be filled. And the really bittersweet awful thing is that he can't even begin to fill the void but he can sort of help her forget that she has it. And he's so in love with her, and he will just lay that on the line. Even if she doesn't want him, he just wants her to be happy. It's sort of one of those classically awful 'just a friend' things."

—KRISTEN STEWART, ACTOR

Bella (Kristen Stewart) stuck between two suitors: Mike (Michael Welch) and Jacob (Taylor Lautner).

Graham Greene as Harry Clearwater.

Kristen Stewart's hair was "mostly her own hair," key hairstylist Thom McIntyre said. Although the hair was styled much as it was in *Twilight*, Bella's varied hairstyles reflect the emotional range of the story, beginning with the happy, optimistic atmosphere that opens the film. "In the first part of the movie her hair is sort of fairy-tale looking, curly and girlish," McIntyre explained. "Then she goes through degrees of it being unkempt after Edward leaves her. As she comes out of her depression, her hair becomes relaxed and carefree, more of a soft wave."

In addition to Taylor Lautner's personal bulking up regimen, key makeup artist Norma Hill-Patton helped add to the illusion of the massive physical growth Jacob undergoes as he becomes a member of the "wolf pack." "For Jacob, the illusion I wanted to create was that suddenly, in a couple of days of story time, he goes from a sweet, innocent young boy to this hunk of a man. I first made Taylor look very fresh, young, and innocent, giving him very smooth skin, with no circles under his eyes, and added a bloom of youth on his cheeks.

"But then, as he changes, he becomes more bronzed and tanned, the look of his face more sculpted. The natural shadow that everyone has I left under his eyes, and I shadowed his nose and cheekbones, his jawline, gave him a slight beard shadow. I defined his eyeline, making them smudgy and smoky-looking, used mascara on his eyebrows to make them black and spiky. We did that to the entire wolf pack, actually. The boys had worked hard on beefing up their bodies and we helped enhance that."

In addition to Lautner's Jacob, the wolf pack included actor Chaske Spencer as Sam Uley (who, in *New Moon*, is leader of the pack), Kiowa Gordon as Embry Call, Bronson Pelletier as Jared, and Alex Meraz as Paul. Other Native American cast members included Gil Birmingham as Billy Black (Jacob's father), Tinsel Korey as Emily, and veteran performer Graham Greene as Harry Clearwater.

Assisting Weitz and head casting director Joseph Middleton was Rene Haynes, a non-native person who has nonetheless developed an expertise in casting Native American roles, with a résumé that ranges from *Dances with Wolves* to

"The way you see the Cullens [the actors] walking around in their wardrobe, and the way their scenes are all set up, it's all very reserved. But there's something about the wolves, even when they're in a short scene, that makes it such a different movie. The wolf pack guys were like a lot of energy, they were always doing dance-off matches and wolf cries. It's a completely new world that has been introduced, and it's warm and fun and a little more frisky. It's also more violent and animalistic in a way that vampires aren't."

—KRISTEN STEWART, ACTOR

Kiowa Gordon practices howling.

The New World. Ultimately, hers was the charge of any casting director—find the best performer for a particular part.

"My office [Rene Haynes Casting] has developed a rapport with native peoples," Haynes explained. "Casting for *New Moon* was fantastic, because we don't get opportunities that often for young Native American actors to appear in something with the following of the TWILIGHT series. And we looked all over North America; it was a huge open casting call."

The popularity of the film series was underscored by the response—20,000 e-mails for the *New Moon* roles flooded in to Haynes and her assistants Jeff Ham and Joanne Brooks. "I have a great compassion for young native actors and we make it our business to find new faces for all our films," Haynes added. "Even though a lot of actors weren't right for *New Moon*, I made notes—this was an amazing new talent pool."

Tyson Houseman, a young Cree from Alberta, Canada, who relocated to Vancouver in hopes of pursing an acting career, was told of the open casting call for *New Moon* by a friend who urged him to give it a try. Like other future members of the wolf pack, he had only a vague knowledge of the TWILIGHT world, and arrived at an intimidating scene. "There were hundreds of people at this open casting call, all real die-hard fans," Houseman recalled. "When I first got the role I didn't think about the fan base. Then somebody told me, 'Do you realize there are thousands of teenage girls that are gonna be freaking out about this?' I was like, 'This is gonna be a little weird.' [laughs] But it's not a bad thing."

Ultimately, he won the role of Quil. Even though Quil doesn't turn into a werewolf until ECLIPSE, Houseman took part in physical work-outs with the other wolf pack actors, a regimen that proved to be a bonding experience. Even on set, the wolf pack competed in push-up and pull-up contests, honing the physical edge that is integral to their characters. "We bonded together because of those workout sessions; we had trainers keep us in shape," noted Chaske Spencer, a Lakota Sioux who, as Sam, was leader of the pack. "We were a band of brothers and the wolf pack had this great chemistry."

"I like to think of us as family," reflected

Bronson Pelletier, a part Cree, part French actor who played Jared. "I have a lot of brothers myself, so I could relate to the character through that."

Chaske Spencer was another who had auditioned without knowing a lot about THE TWILIGHT SAGA, although his nieces informed him "this was a pretty big deal." Through the audition process he prepared by lifting weights for the physical side of the character, and by immersing himself in the mythology through the novel and screenplay. "It's such a good story—it's a werewolf love story," Spencer declared. "This movie is something like Greek tragedy. There's the love triangle between the three main characters, and all these different supporting characters around them. There's action, love, loss, fights, and battle scenes—it's what we go to the movies for.

"I found myself relating to Sam a lot, putting things from my own past into his

Emily (Tinsel Korey) feeds hungry wolves Embry (Kiowa Gordon) and Jared (Bronson Pelletier).

character," Spencer added. "I think Sam is a person that's been thrown into extraordinary circumstances. He's had to sacrifice a lot. Sam is like the chief of police. He's taken on the mantle to be the protector and help guide the other boys who are going through the traumatic experience [of becoming] werewolves, because there was no one there to guide him along. Bella and Jacob's relationship is not a good thing for Sam. She's in love with a vampire, and it's thrown a wrench into what he's trying to do to protect his people."

The wolf pack was thrust into the spotlight early when the actors participated in photo sessions for Summit's *New Moon* promotional campaign. For Spencer, there was the déjà vu sensation of living the kind of pop phenomenon he had grown up on. "It was so much fun. It was like being a kid again, like you're in *Star Wars* or something like that."

Ultimately, the wolf pack appreciated the chance to portray members of the Quileute tribe, a rare opportunity to faithfully present a native people in a popular feature film. "As a Native American it's a great honor to take on a role that is not a stereotype," Spencer reflected. "We don't all have long hair and wear a breech-cloth; we're not all medicine men. This is more contemporary, you can show a different side to our people. It shows us as human beings—who happen to be werewolves."

"AS A NATIVE AMERICAN, IT'S A GREAT HONOR TO TAKE ON A ROLE THAT IS NOT A STEREOTYPE."

The La Push cliff dive scenes were great examples of "invisible effects," when the shot is so convincing that the audience assumes what they are seeing had been shot on a set or on location. That cliff where wolf pack leader Sam Uley is diving had to be a real place, right? "We ended up creating the cliff-diving sequences with three different environments that we shot and composited together," Susan MacLeod said. "It was quite a puzzle to put together.

"Actually, Sam's dive was one of the moments for me when the stars aligned and the final shot looked exactly like the previz. He's shot upside down, it's this impossible camera move. For the greenscreen element of Sam we had a [stunt] guy jump off a seventy-foot tower at the studio in Vancouver. We built a huge, ninety-foot-tall greenscreen and a camera rig that basically descended more or less at the rate of gravity and which also had to do a pan and tilt move. The camera had to drop at the right time, the diver had to dive over it and into the air bag safely, while the camera's pan and tilt orientation followed the movement."

J.J. Makaro talked about when stuntman Lloyd Adams made his dangerous dive off the platform they'd built on a tower at the studio. "Lloyd actually began as a professional dancer, and he translated that ability into gymnastics and began doing high falls into air bags—he's a great 'high fall guy.'"

For Bella's own fateful dive, actress Kristen Stewart's plunge included water scenes shot at an outdoor municipal swimming pool in Vancouver. Prime Focus built bits of a cliff set around the pool, with greenscreen backing around and

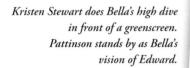

Kristen Stewart does Bella's high dive in front of a greenscreen. Pattinson stands by as Bella's vision of Edward.

in the pool to allow them to digitally extend the cliffs and create murky water below her and an expanse of water beyond. The water at the foot of the cliffs was choppy, thanks to the physical effects department, which stirred things up.

"The physical effects team created a really nice rig for creating turmoil in the water, including a huge dump tank to dump thousands of gallons of water into the swimming pool to create these big waves that batter her around,"

Pascarelli said. "It got pretty rough, and Kristen had to be in that and was a real trouper."

"Kristen is very physically adept, but she doesn't like the water that much and it was a busy and physical day in that pool," explains Makaro. "We had big wave machines and this tank dumping tons of water on her. It was kind of a scary thing, so we trained with her in the pool for a couple weeks, because a lot of the scene happens underwater."

"We taught Kristen about working with the water, and had her in scuba gear, which also gave her something to do that was out of the norm and helped her forget she was in this water environment. It might sound fun to people, being in a pool, but it was springtime and although the pool was heated, the air was crisp, and there was a lot of getting in and out, and they're pounding you with water, and you're treading water all day. She really worked hard. I was impressed."

—J.J. MAKARO, STUNT COORDINATOR

Bella (Kristen Stewart) confronts the wolf pack and
Paul (Alex Meraz) gets in her face.

The werewolves themselves, as described in Meyer's novel, should be wolves the size of small horses. "Making the wolves: that was task number one when I came aboard," visual effects supervisor and producer MacLeod explained. "The great thing is they are wolves, not the iconic bipedal creatures with fur growing out of their hands and face, but are always on all fours. But they can 'phase,' or shape-shift, from human to wolf very quickly. Creating that is not easy to do!"

For Chris Weitz, effects work on *New Moon* was a reunion of sorts. His team on *The Golden Compass*, in addition to Susan MacLeod, had included Tippett Studio (which also did CG wolves for *Golden Compass*) and visual effects supervisor Mike Fink, a veteran visual effects supervisor who won an Academy Award for his work on that film and now headed Prime Focus.

"I've been to that strange planet," the director said, reflecting on the curious challenge of visual effects. "I found on *Golden Compass* that following the visual effects process, from development to final delivery, is a very specific kind of filmmaking that not many people have experienced, especially on a large scale. It means the postproduction period, which is normally about sitting around and, in a very meditative fashion, opining about what cuts you're going to do, has this added element—even though you're not shooting through a camera, you're still making

"THEY CAN 'PHASE,' OR SHAPE-SHIFT, FROM HUMAN TO WOLF VERY QUICKLY. CREATING THAT IS NOT EASY TO DO!"

shots! That is a huge shock. Modern visual effects is a school of contemporary filmmaking of a certain kind."

In hiring Tippett Studio to create the werewolves, the production was also touching the lineage of a storied visual effects tradition. Phil Tippett has won two Emmy Awards and two Academy Awards. Recently, his studio has worked on everything from the monster in *Cloverfield* to the chipmunk in *Enchanted*.

"Tippett Studio was a no-brainer for me. I've worked with them for ten to twelve years, and their strength is animated characters," MacLeod said. "They had an availability and an interest, so it was a match made in heaven. Phil has been doing character animation since before people did it in computers."

The pre-computer animation to which MacLeod refers is the venerable art of "stop motion," an art form and craft that still flourishes in animated films, but was once the means for creating fantastical creatures in live action films (such as the granddaddy monster of them all, King Kong). But everything changed when the digital dinosaurs of *Jurassic Park* hit theaters in 1993. The hand-crafted puppets of old couldn't compete with the photo-realism of computer graphics animation. By then Tippett, who had worked on *Star Wars* and later headed up the ILM creature shop, had his own studio and was working with ILM on a fusion of stop motion and digital technology to

> "We had less than half the time we had on *Golden Compass* to make furry creatures that looked photo-real. For the technology part, we weren't developing the wheel, but we still had to build like a real body, a skeleton with layers of muscle and fat, with skin and fur on top of that, and it all had to move naturally and look real. All of that doesn't come at the press of a button."
>
> —SUSAN MACLEOD, VISUAL EFFECTS SUPERVISOR AND PRODUCER

Director Chris Weitz, visual effects supervisor Susan MacLeod, and Phil Tippett of Tippett Studio.

animate those CG dinosaurs. Ever since, Tippett Studio has brought a hands-on tradition of craft and fantasy storytelling to the creatures they conjure in the digital realm.

The wolf work included shooting "plates," the photographic imagery into which CG creations are integrated, during principal photography with both Weitz's first unit and the second unit helmed by Phil Neilson. The plates were shot in VistaVision, a special widescreen format camera with a film negative twice the size of normal 35-millimeter film. (Developed by Paramount in the 1950s, the first VistaVision release was 1954's *White Christmas*. Eventually abandoned, it was resurrected in the 1970s for *Star Wars* and became the indispensable format for visual effects.)

Susan MacLeod first organized a previz team to develop the wolf shots. The wolf incarnations of Jacob, Sam, Paul, Embry, and Jared were further researched with photographic wolf references from books and online sources. "We started casting the wolves based on the pictures, which we narrowed down to our favorites. We'd pick the body type of one and the fur of the other, and then cut and paste," MacLeod explained.

Tippett Studio had to be involved throughout principal photography. "There are many reasons for us to be on set," added Tippett Studio co-visual effects supervisor Matt Jacobs. "Since we're working with wolves the size of horses, we had to block out the shots so the director, camera crew, and actors knew what they were acting to—after all, the wolf is not there when they're filming."

As visual reference, the effects team used full-scale aluminum and board wolf cutouts weighing twenty to thirty pounds and which had a hole in the side to allow someone to slip

Matt Jacobs

Wolf cutouts were used on set to show where the CG wolf would be in the finished scene.

their arm through and carry the cutouts around during on-camera rehearsals, roughing out with the basic action that had been decided. In addition to four cutouts, there was a wolf's head on a pole that served as the fifth wolf and was used when dynamic action was needed to be blocked out. "We'd grab whoever was available to block out the shots," Jacobs said. "Once we had that reference and gone through rehearsals, we'd pull the cutouts and they'd roll the camera for real. When we got home, having that stand-in was important [as a reference] to our animators."

Tippett artists also had to collect location data for their match move department so that their eventual virtual camera work on the CG wolves would be in perfect sync with the live action camera moves. Devin Breese of Tippett's match move department was set-survey/data supervisor and, in that capacity, used a land surveying tool to record the shooting location's topography and reference marks they could track to. "Back in our shop, we could then match the lens, getting the markers in the right point

in the background plate to track to," explained Ken Kokka, Tippett's producer for the film. "Match movers are critical to our process. They put [the survey data] into the computer and create a set from that."

"Editing visual effects was fun and kind of weird," recalled editor Peter Lambert. "They'd shoot a shot of Bella racing and then there'd be a plate where all you'd see was an empty field where the wolves are supposed to be. It can seem kind of absurd [before a CG wolf is composited]. I'd add temporary sound effects, like wolves howling and scuffling, to make it come alive. The visual effects guys animated based on the timings and angles I'd chosen, so they'd know not to animate a scene at eight seconds, if we were only going to use five."

To further prepare, the Tippett artists studied wolf culture, a strict hierarchical social order ranging from alpha status at the top, to the betas, who are usually hunters, and omega wolves on the bottom.

"Sam is the alpha wolf in the story," Matt Jacobs explained. "Sam is also the biggest guy in stature; he shape-shifts into a black wolf. In our own layouts of the wolves we tried to give them some of the characteristics of the actors playing them, so Sam is going to be a little bit bigger than the rest. Paul is more muscular, so he was slightly wider and more aggressive. Embry was thinner, so we made him a little smaller.

"Between all of them we made different

"The hate that werewolves and vampires have for each other goes way back. The treaty is the most important thing, Jacob is always reminding the vampires about the treaty. So we have the scene at the end [of *New Moon*] where Jacob, Bella, and Edward are together and Jacob's getting kicked out. Edward is about to leave with Bella and Jacob reminds Edward, one last time, 'Remember the treaty.'"

—TAYLOR LAUTNER, ACTOR

colors and markings. For us, it was important to make Jacob extremely iconic. His color is russet brown, basically a reddish-brown color, and in the animation he had to carry himself with an air of pride and nobility."

In February of 2009, a group of Tippett artists got a look at the real thing. "Since they were supposed to be photo-real wolves, my goal was to get the [department] heads in front of a real wolf," Jacobs explained. "I found a place called Wolf Mountain Sanctuary outside Los Angeles. They have a rescue program for wolves, such as wolves that have been pets and have been abandoned. There are pens with, basically, small packs of wolves that cohabitate."

One of those who found the research trip invaluable was animation supervisor Tom Gibbons. "The paradigm of what we do is actually closer to the way Walt Disney started off, where he made animators sit in a room with the actual animal they were going to be stylizing. We always start from a base of reality, whether

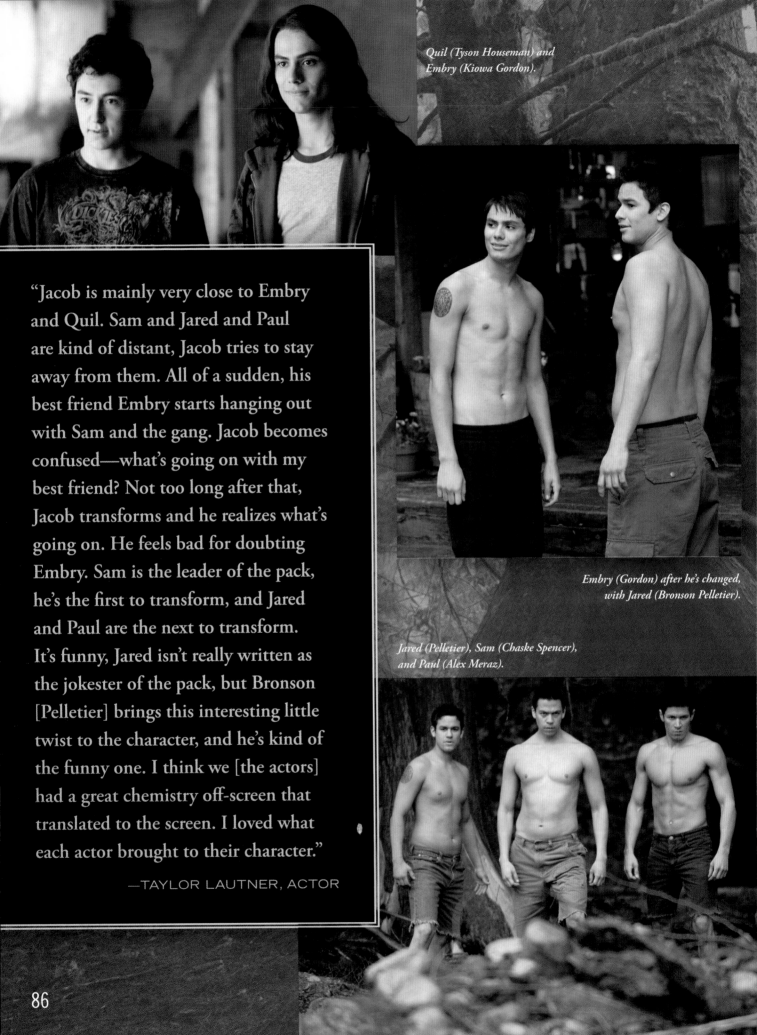

Quil (Tyson Houseman) and Embry (Kiowa Gordon).

"Jacob is mainly very close to Embry and Quil. Sam and Jared and Paul are kind of distant, Jacob tries to stay away from them. All of a sudden, his best friend Embry starts hanging out with Sam and the gang. Jacob becomes confused—what's going on with my best friend? Not too long after that, Jacob transforms and he realizes what's going on. He feels bad for doubting Embry. Sam is the leader of the pack, he's the first to transform, and Jared and Paul are the next to transform. It's funny, Jared isn't really written as the jokester of the pack, but Bronson [Pelletier] brings this interesting little twist to the character, and he's kind of the funny one. I think we [the actors] had a great chemistry off-screen that translated to the screen. I loved what each actor brought to their character."

—TAYLOR LAUTNER, ACTOR

Embry (Gordon) after he's changed, with Jared (Bronson Pelletier).

Jared (Pelletier), Sam (Chaske Spencer), and Paul (Alex Meraz).

we're making a giant robot or a giant wolf. Jacob is our hero, he's Bella's best friend, and he's in love with her, so when he changes he retains that emotional connection with her in wolf form. For this movie, we lifted the wolf behavior from timber wolves and pulled from the actors who transform."

Wolf Mountain had both timber wolves and arctic wolves who ran in packs of three to five. "Wolf behavior across all breeds is similar, and it was fascinating to watch the societal language of the wolf pack and be part of it," Gibbons said.

The idea, Tippett explained, was to give everyone a deeper feeling of the creature they were creating. "I believe that, with animation, you have to put your mind in the space of this character," he concluded.

Ken Kokka took the producer's reins for production. "The main model was Jacob's wolf, all the other variants were based on the Jacob wolf," Kokka explained of the five CG wolves they had to make. "Jacob was our hero, a proud wolf and protector. We thought of these creatures as characters, and Chris and Susan were clear in defining them in those terms."

The "wolf build" at Tippett Studio involved everything from previz work to building the model for the animators. The paint department would paint the fur, effects animators created fur

Sam finds Bella in the woods.

dynamics, and the CG characters and their environments would be match-moved and composited, with proper lighting, by technical directors.

For art director Nate Fredenburg, the challenge of replicating a real creature was the "constant push-pull" between realism and dramatic effect. "Phil is very much about throwing off realism in favor of what makes a dynamic picture, what to put in a shot to create a sense of drama and theater and still have it first with real human characters."

In the design phase, Fredenburg created 2-D paintings and key art as guidelines for the artists, including details for both fur color and groom.

"Wolves are bigger than you think, a couple hundred pounds of muscle. But I was actually much more comfortable with them than if I met a stray dog on the street."

—TOM GIBBONS, TIPPETT STUDIO, ANIMATION SUPERVISOR

Snowdon's design in two colors and one.

Production designer David Brisbin was asked to come up with a tattoo motif for the wolf pack that would be respectful to the Quileute tribe. When Brisbin visited the tribe in Washington, he heard a storyteller reel off a series of tales from Quileute lore and therein found his inspiration.

"One thread that really stuck in my mind referenced the twinning of the wolf character having to do with 'strength in togetherness,'" explained Brisbin. "This fit so well with our story that I ran it by Chris [Weitz] and he agreed to consider a double wolf motif." Vancouver tattoo artist Iesza Snowdon was hired to create the intricate design. From the six variations she created in both black and red, Weitz chose one in just black. To further reinforce the concept of unity, each member of the wolf pack wears the same tattoo.

Alex Meraz gets into character.

Anyone unfamiliar with the process of CG animation who had a chance to look over an animator's shoulder during their werewolf performance work might have found a bewildering array on the computer monitor: visual pull-up references of wolf footage, and 3-D wolf figures of wire mesh moving on a wire mesh set.

Jack Kim, the lead CG modeler on *New Moon*, built the "hero" 3-D model of Jacob's wolf. "They put a muscle system into the wolves that gives the appearance of muscles firing and flexing, as opposed to being rigid," Matt Jacobs explained. "Jack laid out the initial path for how long the hair would be on the wolf, as well as the directional flow of the hair. From there we had our in-house fur software fill in the wolf. From the model department, that initial fur layout went to the painters who were responsible for the color and groom of the fur. This included the markings—in Jacob's case, it's a reddish color with that strange black bandit mask look around the eyes. The painters also added characteristics to the fur. For example, if it was a wet environment, you want to see the hair clump together. They refined the look, before passing it off to the lighting and technical directors.

"We also had procedural simulations create secondary animation characteristics to the fur. For example, if a wolf jumped off a log and hit the ground, that fur had to react to the force, we had to see the fur move. . . . To get that secondary animation, we put an external shell on the wolf. It was invisible, but went around the wolf and created movement and spring on the tips of fur, making for a more natural follow-through."

Tom Gibbons, who supervised the work of about ten animators on an estimated sixty werewolf shots, wanted to avoid getting *too* close to reality. "The way a wolf really snarls, with its front teeth, there's a visceral, primitive, lizard-brain reaction we humans have—*whoa, get back!*

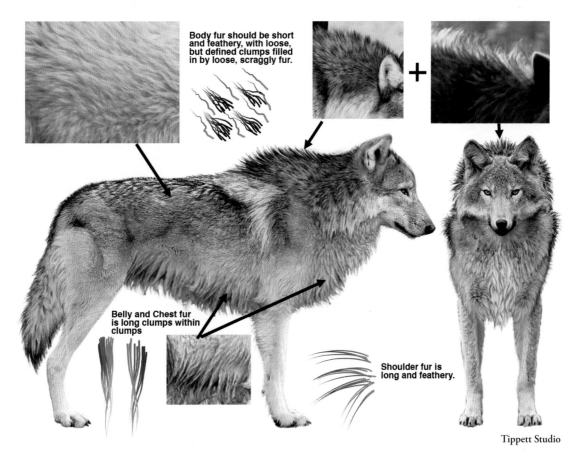

Body fur should be short and feathery, with loose, but defined clumps filled in by loose, scraggly fur.

Belly and Chest fur is long clumps within clumps

Shoulder fur is long and feathery.

Tippett Studio

"Since they're fighting vampires, how big can we make the paws, how long can we make the teeth and keep it in the realm of a real wolf? But we are really good at working from nature and good observers of real animals. It comes naturally to us."

—NATE FREDENBURG, TIPPETT STUDIO, ART DIRECTOR

The final CG wolf placed in the scene.

Tippett Studio

Wolf model placed in the scene.

Tippett Studio

We tried to find a balance, because when they snarl a wolf can look very demonic. We had the writer [to consider], as the role of these wolves is that of sentinels, protectors of the humans. We couldn't make these wolves too aggressive from what the writer intended, and that's part of the collaboration."

To seal the illusion of supernatural wolves interacting with a real environment, CG inter-active elements were created to blend into the composite final image, including computer generated branches to brush back as a wolf passed, sticks, and ground elements to sell the weight of creatures as big as horses.

A dramatic first scene of Jacob phasing into a werewolf begins with the actor in a dramatic leap and ends with his CG werewolf. For the live action work, stunt coordinator J.J. Makaro counted himself lucky to have Taylor Lautner. "Taylor is a really talented kid in physical movement, he is a martial artist and has great body awareness. We utilized him throughout the movie."

The actor was outfitted with a harness that had pick points for wires so the stunt team could "fly" him (with any visible wires removed digitally). "This is not something you could re-create at home," Makaro noted. "We shot outdoors and usually had a couple cranes with wires strung between them and pulleys we would attach and a ratchet, which is a pneumatic ram that acts like a deadweight to send you flying through the air."

For the stunt in which Jacob bounds over Bella to transform, the actor not only had to hit his mark, but also freeze in midair at the point where he would instantly transform into a werewolf. The rigging was "a web of cables" that slowed the actor down and helped him freeze

in midair, but Lautner also had to time his leap over Kristen Stewart. "We had to take him over the top of her, so we're hitting buttons, and had to time it so he could get enough height over her," Makaro explained. "But Taylor had to push off to fly, and if he's not in the right spot…it gets twitchy, he could run right into her. But after rehearsals, he nailed it every time. He was a natural—he'd make a hell of a stuntman!"

"When Jacob phases into a werewolf, Chris wanted Jacob's face to be pretty dramatic on the fly," elaborated Susan MacLeod. "I said it would be great to put him on a wire rig to have him leap in the air and pose and we'll transform him. We prevized that because there was a lot that had to happen at the same time—the camera had to move twenty feet per second on its z axis, so it had to pull back at twenty feet per second to follow the leap through the air, it's panning and tilting and the stunt had to happen at the precise moment.

"Taylor, who did the stunt, had to hit his mark. The stunt rig, which was built by the special effects department, had to lift Taylor

Tippett Studio

The progression of the computer model, from muscle system to the mesh guide for the fur.

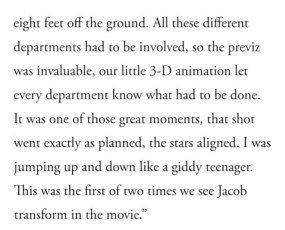

> "What's special about Jacob is he's the only one who transforms in midair. I had my harness on and wires for when I take off and run and jump over Bella, and they jolted me in midair and I stopped—I had to freeze—because then they convert my body into the wolf's body. It's just me, a human, running and leaping into the air—poof! The clothes shred and fly off and I land as a wolf."
>
> —TAYLOR LAUTNER, ACTOR

eight feet off the ground. All these different departments had to be involved, so the previz was invaluable, our little 3-D animation let every department know what had to be done. It was one of those great moments, that shot went exactly as planned, the stars aligned. I was jumping up and down like a giddy teenager. This was the first of two times we see Jacob transform in the movie."

"I did martial arts for about eight years," said Lautner, "so that was kind of helpful [in doing physical stunts]. The big thing with Jacob is that, pretransformation, he's very clumsy. Bella has always known him as this clumsy little kid. He's tripping over his own feet, so I had to bring that into the character. But as soon as he transforms, he's extremely agile."

Tippett Studio was still in the very early stages of Jacob's CG transformation when a theatrical trailer of *The Twilight Saga: New Moon* got moved up so it could be unveiled at the MTV Movie Awards in June 2009. Tippett Studio executive producer Kip Larsen recalled it was April 17 when they were first asked by the production if they could deliver a CG wolf by May 22. The decision to move ahead was made five days later, leaving a month to do the shot. "We didn't start our wolf build until March, so we were nervous when they moved up the trailer," producer Kokka said. "But we pooled our resources and delivered a shot. The deadline actually gave everyone a clear focus, it forced us to make something good and accelerated the entire process."

"There were a lot more issues to prove out, like the speed for the transitions when people phase from human to wolf," Phil Tippett added. "Because of the rush we couldn't do some detail things, like having steam rise off the animals, or sweat, all the things that bring a shot to life. All those details got thrown out, and we came back to them later. The trailer was our dress rehearsal."

"For the phasing, the director wasn't interested in a slow transformation, but something instantaneous and explosive," Nate Fredenburg said. "It's a pretty fluid movement from human to wolf—it happens in eight to ten frames."

"The production provided us the Vista-Vision plate for reframing, which included all the actors," Larsen explained. "Jacob was attached to a wire rig which assisted his leap. That rig was digitally removed from the plate and we also replaced the actor with a CG version of himself three frames prior to his leap. The transformation from human to wolf takes place in midair using CG versions of the actor and the wolf."

A few weeks after the MTV event, Ken Kokka got an e-mail alert that there had been an estimated ten million downloads of the trailer. "That opened our eyes," he reflected. "This was a real phenomenon, we were part of a cultural happening."

Jacob grabs some sleep after running through the woods all night as a wolf.

93

A Moonless Night

Robert Pattinson as Edward Cullen.

Laurent (Edi Gathegi) is back and this time he's hungry.

New Moon delves deeper into the vampire world, giving filmmakers an opportunity to explore it with new eyes.

In *The Twilight Saga: New Moon*, costume designer Tish Monaghan created a different look for the "feral vampires" Laurent and Victoria, from the wanderers that appeared in *Twilight*. "Our director wanted a more elegant look, less rock and roll," Monaghan explained.

Any stylistic difference from the first film was easily explained—Laurent and Victoria wear the clothing and personal effects of their victims. "The understanding is Victoria and Laurent are on a killing spree," Monaghan said. "We wanted their costumes to make sense, story-wise, but also to look good on screen and fit into the color world. For Victoria we had a bit more stylish look, not so earthy. For their 'silhouette,' meaning the shape of the garment against the body, I wanted a flow because she's doing things like running through the woods and diving into water, and I wanted to see bits of fabric trailing behind her, so that her clothes have movement.

For Laurent, actor Edi Gathegi asked if he could be bare-chested under his jacket, as in *Twilight*. But the costume designer traded in the character's old leather jacket for something nicer. "For Laurent it was a complete switch. I turned to runway fashion models for inspiration and Italian clothing lines."

The makeup for Laurent was also different. "I liked the idea that he looked more like a vampire, with pale skin, which we didn't see the last time," Hill-Patton said.

From the visual effects side, there were also key "vampire effects," as Susan MacLeod called them. "Although we couldn't do CG vampires because of time constraints, there was a desire to emphasize their supernatural nature with the illusion of super speed, and do it in-camera. I pulled speed effect references and put together a reel, but it didn't look right, it seemed herky-jerky and silly. What we really liked was slow motion, which, in some way, was really

THE MEADOW LOCATION
BECAME AN EXAMPLE
OF THE DIFFICULTY OF
SHOOTING IN A REGION
WITH SOMETIMES
UNPREDICTABLE WEATHER.

evocative and provided a sense of hyperreality. What slow motion did, I think, was put you into their world."

To achieve slow motion requires shooting at a considerably higher frame rate than the normal twenty-four frames per second. In preproduction, there was a "proof of concept test," MacLeod noted, which they shared with the production, particularly the second unit in charge of filming stunts and action scenes. "We came up with a recipe for vampire speed. The rule of thumb was to shoot at ninety-six frames per second, but the light often didn't allow for that, especially in the forest. So, the minimum was forty-eight frames per second."

For Bella, a fateful return to the meadow where she was first bedazzled by Edward's glittering vampire skin becomes a nightmare as Laurent appears, eager to taste the flesh of this sweet mortal—until Jacob, with his wolf pack, suddenly arrives to save her.

"The plan for the meadow sequence was to carry it out with a Steadicam traveling while on Bella, through three hundred sixty degrees to Laurent," Aguirresarobe said. "The natural light varied in intensity during the one-minute sequence, but in spite of some difficulties, I was lucky with the weather and the time, resulting in the finished sequence feeling extraordinary."

The meadow location became an example of the difficulty of shooting in a region with sometimes unpredictable weather. Although Vancouver did not seem to elicit the horror stories of elemental forces that bedeviled the *Twilight* shoot in Portland, there were moments when the production had to go to what line producer Bill Bannerman calls "Plan B."

"Consistency of weather was a challenge on this movie," Bannerman explained. "But there is a *Twilight* signature that is crucial, of dismal damp and overcast, because the vampires can't be in direct sunlight. So you have to prepare for the unpredictable elements where the shooting might change five times in one day. For example, we had a scene in the pristine meadow, which was supposed to be lush and full of vegetation. The day we were going to shoot there it was

pouring rain. Then it began snowing, and didn't stop snowing for three hours."

Undaunted, the production packed up and within an hour was at Plan B—a storage structure a football field's length from the meadow, where Bella's truck was set up on a greenscreen stage. Without wasting the snow day, the production got a shot of Lautner and Stewart on the drive to the diving cliffs of La Push (a "poor man's process," as Bannerman adds, with the environment in which they're supposed to be traveling added later). "I have a Plan B, C, D, and E," Bannerman chuckled. "You just have to be calm and collected. The more experience you have, the more you anticipate every possible scenario for what could happen. I live by the motto a professor once told me: 'If you fail to plan, you plan to fail!'"

Victoria is a menacing presence throughout, and gets chased by Charlie's hunting party, a group who has plunged into the forest seeking a wild predatory creature—without realizing they are actually hunting a vampire. The scenes were shot in a real forest, with actress Rachelle

"In this movie, Victoria is sort of waiting in the wings. It would be interesting to see what she is going through, because she has lost her mate and wants to kill me because of that. It's like, Edward shouldn't have his mate if she can't have hers, so she's after me the entire time. There's a lot of POVs in the forest, it's like I'm constantly being watched. Thank goodness Jacob is a werewolf and not some nice kid, because he needs to defend my life while Edward is away."

—KRISTEN STEWART, ACTOR

Rachelle Lefevre returns as Victoria.

Lefevre volunteering for all the wire rig flying tricks J.J. Makaro's team could design for her character's crazed leaps from tree to tree.

"All the actors on this show wanted to do what their characters were doing and as many stunts as I would allow them to do. They all gave one hundred percent," Makaro said. "For Rachelle's character we were in a real forest and flying twelve to twenty feet. We wanted to avoid a floaty feeling, so she'd leap off a tree and would fly close enough to the next tree to grab it, but you had to play the breaking point, she would get a pretty good knock every time she hit the tree. Rachelle took a pretty good pounding for the team. She had a phenomenal stunt double and they'd test everything. I'd give Rachelle a difficulty scale from one to ten, with one being a walk in the park to ten being that last hit you didn't like so much. I might say, 'This is a seven.' She'd just say, 'Hook me up.' It was really impressive what she was doing."

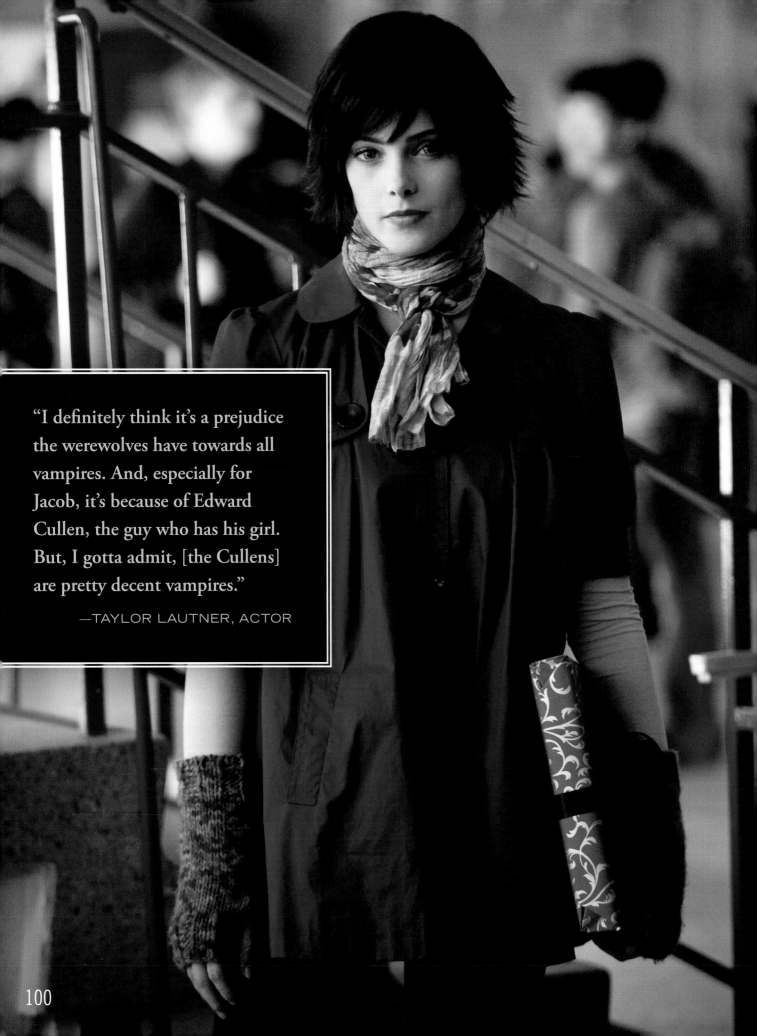

"I definitely think it's a prejudice the werewolves have towards all vampires. And, especially for Jacob, it's because of Edward Cullen, the guy who has his girl. But, I gotta admit, [the Cullens] are pretty decent vampires."

—TAYLOR LAUTNER, ACTOR

"For the Cullens, the new director felt their world [as presented in *Twilight*] was a little too separated, color-wise, from the rest of the people in the town," explained costume designer Tish Monaghan. "He wanted to maintain their cool, gray world, but with a minor shift in the color palette. Rather than pastel hues, he steered me to grays and blues. Of course, the actors had also done a lot of work with the previous designer, and the studio was pleased with their general look, so I jumped on board to honor both the previous discussions from the first movie and what Chris was requesting."

The look of the Cullens themselves remained generally faithful to the first movie, although they received a subtle makeover at the hands of key makeup artist Norma Hill-Patton, whose credits include working on Halle Berry's movies as her personal makeup artist. "When you work with an actor as their personal makeup artist you become more than just a makeup artist," she reflected. "You get to know the actor so well, you become a confidant, a friend, a therapist, a support system. It's good for them to come onto a set on day one, sit down, and there's a shorthand. You know their face so well, what works and doesn't work, what they like and don't like. You have to know all the actors, but there are so many personalities in that trailer, including all the makeup and hair people, that you have to be sympathetic to everyone's needs, right down to choosing the music you listen to.

"The director and I wanted a more translucent look to the vampire skin," Hill-Patton said. "The Cullens, and all the vampire characters, have very pale skin, but I didn't want them stark white and walking amongst the average person, that would be too much for the realm of believability. I had to do the research and look at many, many different types of products and creams and paints to find the look. I was looking for the shade, consistency, and wearability, because the makeup had to be on the actors in

Alice and Bella become close friends in **New Moon.**

Peter Facinelli as
Dr. Carlisle Cullen.

"THE CULLENS, AND
ALL THE VAMPIRE
CHARACTERS, HAVE
VERY PALE SKIN, BUT
I DIDN'T WANT THEM
STARK WHITE AND
WALKING AMONGST
THE AVERAGE PERSON,
THAT WOULD BE TOO
MUCH FOR THE REALM
OF BELIEVABILITY."

Jackson Rathbone
and Ashley Greene
as Jasper Hale and
Alice Cullen.

Nikki Reed and Kellan Lutz as Rosalie Hale and Emmett Cullen.

Elizabeth Reaser as Esme Cullen.

Robert Pattinson as Edward Cullen.

all weather conditions.

"I layered two different tones of makeup, one on top of the other, which gave a depth, not one flat tone. For all the characters, we had to keep repainting the makeup using a fixative, which is a professional spray-on product, to hold the makeup in place so it wouldn't run."

Key hairstylist Thom McIntyre, whose work can be seen in *Seven Years in Tibet*, *Snow Falling on Cedars*, and *Paycheck*, worked closely with Hill-Patton.

"On *New Moon*, we were kind of limited by what was done in the first movie, but we still had to bring to reality Chris and Stephenie's vision, and were given new characters as well," McIntyre said. "The makeup for the vampires was essential, and the hairstyle had to complement it."

There was, McIntyre noted, "extensive wig work" in the film. Nikki Reed, who plays Rosalie Hale, had bleached her hair for *Twilight*, but was fitted with a long blond wig for the new production. The dreadlocks of the vampire Laurent had been a synthetic, machine-made wig in the first film, but this time were made with real human hair. Stacey Butterworth, the wig maker and a key part of McIntyre's team (which included his assistant Gina Sherritt, and Paul Edwards on second unit), crafted each wig by hand.

"T
ROB
TH

Robert Pattinson filmed many of the same scenes as Stewart but with a greenscreen so that Bella's vision of Edward could be added in later.

The process begins by tracing an actor's hairline pattern, then creating a lace base through which each hole is hooked with hair that has been mixed in various colors. After flattening an actor's own hair in place as needed, the wig is then glued on. "Once the wig is made, it has to be cut and styled daily, just like normal hair," McIntyre explained. "At night the lace would be cleaned and the wig blocked to retain the shape of the head."

Throughout the film, Bella's reckless moments summon Edward's spectral presence, a calming influence that helps her pull back

from the brink of danger. "Movies are a visual medium, and the more Rob Pattinson the better, so the idea was to not just hear but see him," Susan MacLeod explained. "But that's not in Stephenie Meyer's book, so we didn't have anything to guide that look development.

"But when I think of an apparition, I think of fluidity. I was thinking of water and Chris gravitated to flame, like Edward is carrying a torch for Bella, which I thought was nice, and flame has a lot of elegant movement and fluidity. We started with that as a touchstone and we selected a lot of flame images, which I turned

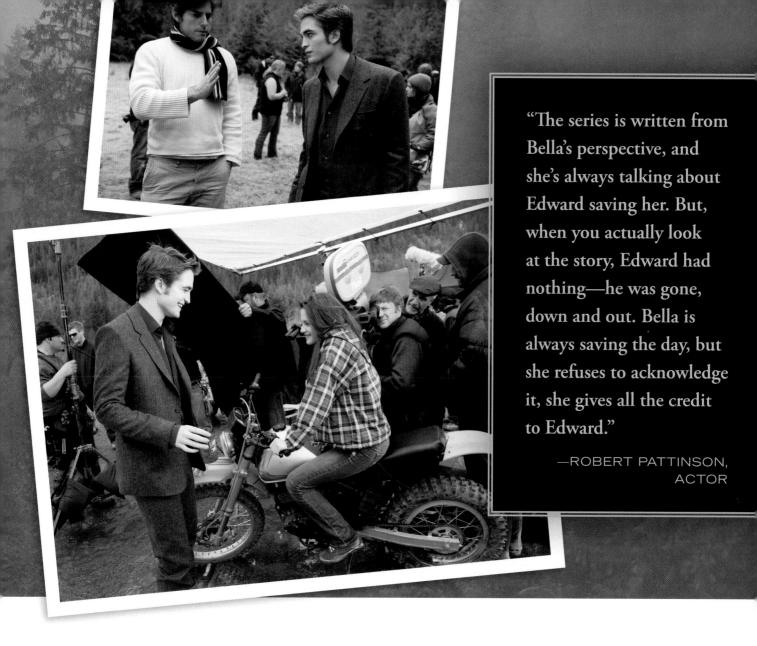

> "The series is written from Bella's perspective, and she's always talking about Edward saving her. But, when you actually look at the story, Edward had nothing—he was gone, down and out. Bella is always saving the day, but she refuses to acknowledge it, she gives all the credit to Edward."
>
> —ROBERT PATTINSON, ACTOR

over to [Prime Focus]."

The effect itself required actor Robert Pattinson to be shot separately against a greenscreen, and the resulting image was composited into the live action scenes and manipulated for the desired effect.

"We had to create this kind of subtle modulation," said visual effects supervisor Pascarelli. "Early on, Susan and I decided to light the greenscreen very carefully to match the lighting in the background plate, otherwise Edward might not look like he's in the same shot. Because some of the shots were moving,

we had to shoot the background plates on dollies and hand-operated cameras and match-move them and output a motion control file so that we could shoot Edward's greenscreen with the matching camera move."

"For ninety percent of the movie, Robert Pattinson appears in the suit he wore at Bella's birthday party," costume designer Monaghan explained. "It's a gray tweed suit, with little flecks of brown, blue, and green. I wanted an old-world quality. In essence it was a suit he might have worn before he became a vampire, we wanted to keep some of that element.

When he disappears, he goes into his own state of mourning, off-camera. Whenever Edward's apparition appears to Bella, he's always wearing that suit, because that's the image she has of him before he left."

Edward's plan to kill himself is an outlandish, in-your-face affront to the Volturi. Edward travels to their secret headquarters town in Volterra, Italy, with plans to step out into the town square at high noon, exposing his flesh to the sun and revealing his vampire nature to the townspeople. There would be several times in the film when the sparkling quality of Edward's vampire skin would be displayed, including an original flashback to the *Twilight* meadow scene, as Pascarelli noted. Prime Focus would have to create the effect, dubbed "diamond guy" by Susan MacLeod. The approach would be a fresh interpretation from what had been seen in the first movie. The

diamond-guy effect was, like the apparition, another subjective creative exploration.

"The diamond-guy effect we weren't one hundred percent sure about, because it's something you've never seen in your life," MacLeod admitted. "So, I collected a lot of images of snow, ice, marble. We knew we would need to match it up precisely to Rob's head with a 3-D effect to match his head movement. Although he had been scanned in the first movie, people's bodies change, so we rescanned him for *New Moon*. Rob is already a beautiful guy, but we wanted to make him gorgeous in the diamond-guy scenes, like sunlight on snow."

"From the scan we did of Robert Pattinson's face, neck, and torso, we created a CG match to the real Edward," Pascarelli explained. "We had to track the overall camera move, then match-move the CG Edward to the real Edward. For the diamond effect, the animators had substrates, or a mesh, on which to seed sparkles motivated by the actor's movement. It was not a glitter effect, but fine detail, these diamond chunks—we had to put the right tracking marks to lock that diamond effect onto his face. The individual particles appear more luminous, what I call 'forceful ballistics,' meaning like a lighthouse where it's dark and then the light comes around to your eyes and goes *pow!*"

> "ROB IS ALREADY A BEAUTIFUL GUY, BUT WE WANTED TO MAKE HIM GORGEOUS IN THE DIAMOND- GUY SCENES, LIKE SUNLIGHT ON SNOW."

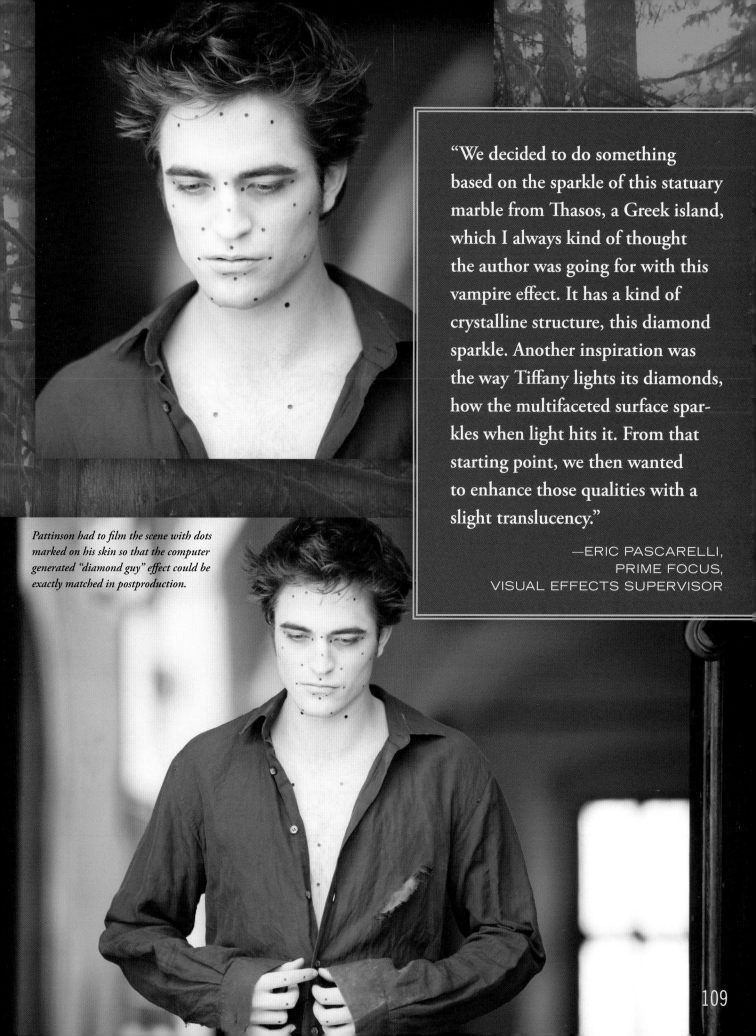

Pattinson had to film the scene with dots marked on his skin so that the computer generated "diamond guy" effect could be exactly matched in postproduction.

"We decided to do something based on the sparkle of this statuary marble from Thasos, a Greek island, which I always kind of thought the author was going for with this vampire effect. It has a kind of crystalline structure, this diamond sparkle. Another inspiration was the way Tiffany lights its diamonds, how the multifaceted surface sparkles when light hits it. From that starting point, we then wanted to enhance those qualities with a slight translucency."

—ERIC PASCARELLI,
PRIME FOCUS,
VISUAL EFFECTS SUPERVISOR

The Coldest Ones

The three leaders of the Volturi, left to right:
Marcus (Christopher Heyerdahl), Aro (Michael Sheen),
and Caius (Jamie Campbell Bower).

Bella's first glimpse of the Volturi is a painting at the Cullen house, which depicts the aristocratic vampires in the 1800s, standing on a balcony and looking down upon a "bacchanalian party scene," as Eric Pascarelli put it. In one of the magical transitions of the film's narrative style, the camera pushes into the painted scene and takes the story back into the past. "We shot the Volturi actors on a balcony set, what would be the top half of the painting," Pascarelli explained. "We took a single frame as our hero frame, and an actual painting was based upon that. It was a very complex shot for us, because the camera pushing in had to blend perfectly into this vertically framed painting and transition to live action."

There would be two looks for the Volturi, one for that scene from the 1800s, another for contemporary time. Each look would emphasize the social order with the highest being Aro, one of the three "ancients," along with Caius and Marcus. "For their eighteenth-century look, I settled on the beginnings of the modern suit, with a slim coat to their knees," Tish Monaghan explained. "They wear breeches and long hose and muslin shirts with a stock around their neck. In the 1800s, Aro is dressed in the lightest clothing of all of them, but in the contemporary world black is the indication of status and power and he's the darkest—as Stephenie Meyer says, 'Aro was the darkest of all.' After Aro, Jane is next, then the Volturi guards Demetri and Felix, who I have in gray scale leaning toward black.

"I saw them as wearing judicial robes, because when we see them in the eighteenth century they're passing judgment. I tried to look at the roots of that type of garment in Tuscany. When they come to life in the painting, they turn and walk down a corridor to the Volturi chamber to pass judgment on a rogue vampire. Their robes are hanging off the back of their chairs and they put them on. That is how they look when Edward encounters them. They're sitting in their chairs, in their judicial robes, [and] we see their clothes underneath. Aro, however, doesn't wear a robe, just a pure black suit."

"The Volturi have had two thousand years to go slightly mad," Chris Weitz reflected. "They have a backstory in that they have retreated to a

"I think two thousand years of living has made [the Volturi] slightly nuts, has led them to think they're practically gods, and has given them a perverse attitude to human life."

—CHRIS WEITZ, DIRECTOR

The town square in Montepulciano, Italy, standing in for Volterra.

"We didn't want to re-create a 3-D model of an Italian town, or shoot the Volturi headquarters as a greenscreen set, which you could do. If you can't achieve realism, you're just hitting the audience with bells and whistles. So we built our interior set in Vancouver and shot the exterior in Montepulciano, Italy, which gave an extraordinary amount of texture that, frankly, no CG could manage to achieve. There's something about environments existing in real space that human beings, even though they're watching it on a 2-D screen, can recognize instantly."

—CHRIS WEITZ, DIRECTOR

life of contemplation and they care about maintaining order in the vampire world. They have their operatives who go out and do things, but it's rare for the three ancients to leave their inner sanctum. As a result, they're paler than the rest [of the vampires], a lot less inclined to violence, although they are dangerous."

The location in Italy not only needed to

be an ancient town, but it had to serve the story as Bella and Alice Cullen drive through ancient cobblestone streets to reach the main square and the clock tower under which Edward plans to step into the noontime sun. Edward has arrived in Italy in a bedraggled state, dressed in the same gray tweed suit he's now worn for months. "From the pristine appearance of the birthday

party, to when we see him in Italy, his suit is now threadbare, he doesn't have his jacket, his pants are dirty, his shoes are scuffed," observed Monaghan, whose team helped age up the suit. "He has been alone and wandering, and is prepared to give up his life at this point."

The scouting team that flew to Italy during the *New Moon* prep period included Wyck Godfrey, Chris Weitz, David Brisbin, Javier Aguirresarobe, and Bill Bannerman. "We went to about twelve different old cities, trying to find the best representation for what Stephenie described in the book, this square with a clock tower," Godfrey recalled. "For the town you want the sense of history and how long the Volturi have lived in their caverns underneath the city. We wanted a place where we could look at side streets and go into buildings, as well as the hero location of the square."

The set for the great marble hall of the Volturi, built on a soundstage in Vancouver, would tie in with the town of Montepulciano in the Tuscany region, which was selected as the perfect stand-in for Volterra, an actual medieval town which Bella first sees and describes in the novel as "ancient sienna walls and towers crowning the peak of the steep hill."[9]

"Volterra had a more medieval aspect, but Montepulciano had more Renaissance influence—and with the Renaissance comes symmetry," Weitz said. "We were also going to save the color red for the end, and the main square had a redbrick floor which we could use for our high shot. And as Alice and Bella race their Porsche to the main square, we had beautiful views of ancient alleyways and roadways that looked out over vineyards and green fields."

"We wanted the feeling you're not in Forks anymore. Bella's small world in Forks, where she's found what she thinks is this odd family, is much bigger than that, the world of vampires all of a sudden blows open."

—WYCK GODFREY, PRODUCER

"I loved Montepulciano. It was a stunning and beautiful way to end the film by going to a place with so much history that is home to the Volturi, who live underground in this big cavern."

—TISH MONAGHAN, COSTUME DESIGNER

"Montepulciano was a beautiful, medieval town, everything was ancient. The actors were quite different when they were there, quite in awe of the space around them. That feeling that this was a different world overtook them and all of us, as well as the desperation of what we had to achieve in the storyline."

—THOM MCINTYRE, KEY HAIRSTYLIST

The "chess game," as Bill Bannerman terms the art of physical production work, had the flavor of a military campaign in its organization, which included going over every inch of a map of Montepulciano to glean all potential logistical problems, right down to the type of tow truck needed to get through a particularly narrow street. Bannerman made a follow-up scout with a *New Moon* Italian unit that handled a lot of the logistics, while the production designer and costume designer also made trips to Italy to prepare. A bed-and-breakfast hotel was secured as the hub for hair, makeup, and costume, and the requisite permissions were obtained.

"The shoot in Italy required a lot of preparation and planning across all departments," Bannerman explained. "The town is a walled city, around 1,500 years old, and on top of a hill. It's less than one square mile and is a very compressed, confined space—all the streets are

"[THE FANS] WERE WONDERFUL AND ADORABLE, BUT AT THE SAME TIME WE NEEDED TO MAKE SURE WE GOT OUR SHOTS."

as wide as a car. When you come to historical towns you have to come in with respect, and this town had so much history, it was an awe-inspiring adventure.

"We wrapped principal photography in Vancouver on a Thursday, and a small component of the Vancouver crew got on a plane that Friday to fly to Italy, and we were shooting on Tuesday. So, prior to that, a lot of intense prep work had to be done so when the cast and director arrived to the set that morning we'd be moving."

As it turned out, the ancient dust would be trod upon not only by a twenty-first century film crew, but by a legion of Twilighters. "It seemed every [fan] from continental Europe had come to Montepulciano." Weitz smiled. "All these narrow streets were filled with young [fans.] They were wonderful and adorable, but at the same time we needed to make sure we got our shots."

Alice (Ashley Greene) tries to keep a low profile in Italy.

Producer Wyck Godfrey and special effects supervisor Susan MacLeod.

Key hairstylist Thom McIntyre recalled one day when the hair, makeup, and costume departments couldn't leave the little hotel that was their base of operations because fans were pressed up against the locked front door. At least, he notes, they didn't break it down, or smash any windows. "The streets had to be cordoned off and the police and bodyguards called in to push the crowds back," McIntyre recalled. "It was a little scary, but also truly amazing. I've seen similar things, but not for years—it was like the Beatles arriving."

There was a bonus to the throng of frantic fans—for the festival that fills the main square, a call for extras got one hundred percent results. The director chuckled that they had to hire older males with beards to mix with a crowd whose "gender composition" was mostly female (and had its collective eye out for every move of Robert Pattinson).

It was, the director admitted, a fortuitous decision to have the festival crowd not only dressed in red, but hooded cloaks. "I had to get 963 costumes ready for the square in Italy, including 850 red hooded cloaks," said Monaghan, who had a six-person crew to complement the eighteen-person department back in Vancouver. "We also rented about thirty Elizabethan costumes. Bella is wearing a dark green shirt and blue jeans and darting through the crowd, running up these cobblestone streets, and when she gets to the square it's filled with people."

Principal photography ended with the conclusion of filming in Montepulciano. Editor Peter Lambert, sitting in front of his Avid digital editing machine, would recall how grand an illusion it was, the way the location footage of the old Tuscan town blended seamlessly with the set erected on a Vancouver soundstage, that representation of the subterranean vampire world flourishing below the cobblestone streets. "You only had to see it a few times to be completely fooled that it was a place in the town."

Gillian Bohrer, Summit's director of development, recalled the day she escorted Stephenie Meyer onto the soundstage for the author's first view of the great Volturi Hall. The actors playing the Volturi appeared, dramatically, to pay their respects.

"For whatever reason, someone had the lights on at the end of the set where the thrones would be, and as the actors walked in they were silhouetted by this light as we stood at the base of the throne. I introduced Stephenie as they walked in, it was really cool. That set was the biggest thing we built for the movie, and it was actually about how Stephenie imagined it—she thinks big!"

Art director Catherine Ircha noted the Volturi set was scheduled for the end of filming in Vancouver, and it was the climactic grand design the production designer kept building toward. "The design process for the Volturi Hall started from day one," she explained.

"It's invigorating to be on a set and create a sensationalized environment. Building a 20,000-square-foot set of a Volturi chamber, and watching vampires fight face-to-face, is not something you do every day."

—BILL BANNERMAN, LINE PRODUCER

"We had thousands of pieces of wood done to look like marble, and we pieced them all in separately on the floor and walls of the great hall."

—CATHERINE IRCHA,
ART DIRECTOR

"I have an architectural background, so the [Volturi] hall was inspired by a variety of pieces. I was aware of the heroes of Tuscan architecture, but it's our own invention. Hopefully it will be a nice surprise for readers who know the space from the book but haven't seen it in visual terms."

—DAVID BRISBIN, PRODUCTION DESIGNER

Well-known actress Dakota Fanning takes on the role of sinister Volturi member Jane.

"Tying the stage we built in Vancouver to existing spaces involved extrapolating what was described in the book and the script to create a space that served the pieces of story that had to be told," Brisbin explained. "There was the sequence where Bella goes into the world of the Volturi, the inner sanctum of inner sanctums. It's not only an unimaginable kind of organization, it's in an unimaginable place where you can't figure out how to get there, how to access it. We wanted to create a space for the Volturi Hall that was a breathtaking surprise, which defied any preconceptions of any dark and spooky vampire world.

"We went with the cues given by Stephenie Meyer that it's sort of a white marble hall. There is a beautiful medieval sensibility in the main square of Montepulciano, so we extrapolated from that to create our own space."

"The Volturi [Hall] was the heart of the film for [David Brisbin] as a design element, this enormous set as big as you can imagine, so tall and wide and massive that when you walked onto that set it took your breath away," said Ircha. "It was about sixty feet wide, forty feet high, with a visual effect element to add another sixty feet or more to the dome, which we also designed. It was a powerful, mammoth space which gave a lot of play for all the actors and gave the Volturi a glamorous and glorious look."

A faux-marble effect was a key part of the Volturi world. "When the Volturi walk from the balcony to the great hall they walk through a field of columns made of wood, but for us, it's made of marble," Ircha said. "David would go, 'I like this green marble with this veining, this gray marble with that veining.' We did a lot of samples of textures and marble—the Duomo in Florence has a lot of the flavor we were after, green tile against cream, or gray, tile. But there were plenty of references. All the samples and aging and texture—he pulled all that together. Two weeks before principal photography started, we worked on marble samples, and by the third week of principal photography, when we shot at the high school, we had marble samples good enough to show Chris and Javier. We had, I'm sure, about one hundred people doing marble for the next three weeks. It was a big job."

Michael Sheen, a respected Welsh actor

known for his lead performances in the Academy Award-nominated films *The Queen* and *Frost/Nixon,* joined *New Moon* to play one of the Volturi leaders. Cast as the powerful Aro, Sheen hailed Meyer's book for the complexity of his character and the Volturi, as well as the opportunity to join the lineage of actors who have interpreted vampires. "In a way, playing a vampire is sort of like playing Hamlet, there have been so many depictions. Aro is dangerous and deadly and powerful, yet the way he's written he doesn't come across as a sinister Dracula character—Stephenie describes his voice in the book as being feathery and like a long sigh. I love the idea that the vampires, generally, as a species are very attractive to their prey. They're the perfect predators, they've evolved to be able to lure their prey, the humans, to them."

"The Volturi are the closest the vampire world

"FOR BELLA, WE TRIED TO CONVEY THE FEELING OF A HUMAN BEING CAUGHT IN THE MIDDLE OF A PACK OF VAMPIRES FIGHTING."

has to royalty, they decide what is right and they enforce the laws," Kristen Stewart said. "Edward wants to kill himself because he thinks Bella killed herself and [we end up] having this big meeting. It's funny, the book says they have no regard for human life, but the way Aro treats Edward and Bella is oddly compassionate."

For the face-off between the Volturi and Edward, Bella, and Alice Cullen, an early draft of the script envisioned a battle royal. "In the book Jane paralyzes Edward, but for the movie we wanted something grander, so I introduced the idea of this battle," Melissa Rosenberg recalled. "I had Edward fighting every Volturi guard in the place, Alice fighting, Edward being flung to the ceiling, vampires being slung around left and right—what I had written was half a movie budget! It's the old story from *Gone With the Wind*: 'And then Atlanta burns.' Stephenie did rein me in, and we settled for

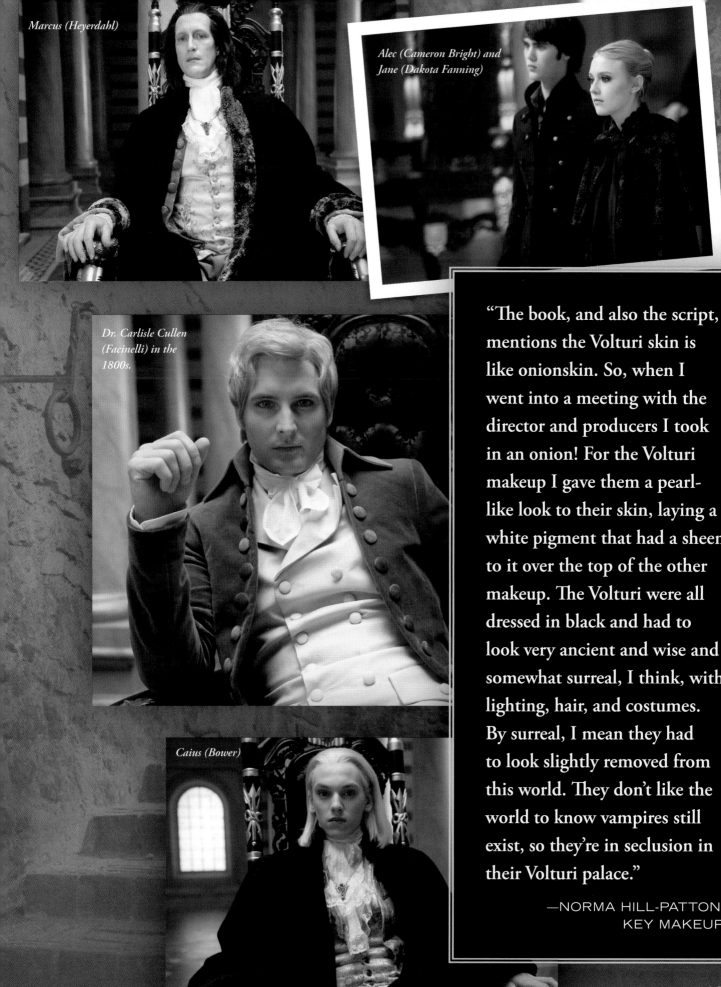

Marcus (Heyerdahl)

Alec (Cameron Bright) and Jane (Dakota Fanning)

Dr. Carlisle Cullen (Facinelli) in the 1800s.

Caius (Bower)

"The book, and also the script, mentions the Volturi skin is like onionskin. So, when I went into a meeting with the director and producers I took in an onion! For the Volturi makeup I gave them a pearl-like look to their skin, laying a white pigment that had a sheen to it over the top of the other makeup. The Volturi were all dressed in black and had to look very ancient and wise and somewhat surreal, I think, with lighting, hair, and costumes. By surreal, I mean they had to look slightly removed from this world. They don't like the world to know vampires still exist, so they're in seclusion in their Volturi palace."

—NORMA HILL-PATTON, KEY MAKEUP

"STEPHENIE POINTED OUT THAT FELIX IS A VOLTURI GUARD, AND HIS GIFT IS FIGHTING, SO THAT WOULD BE ENOUGH OF A CHALLENGE FOR EDWARD."

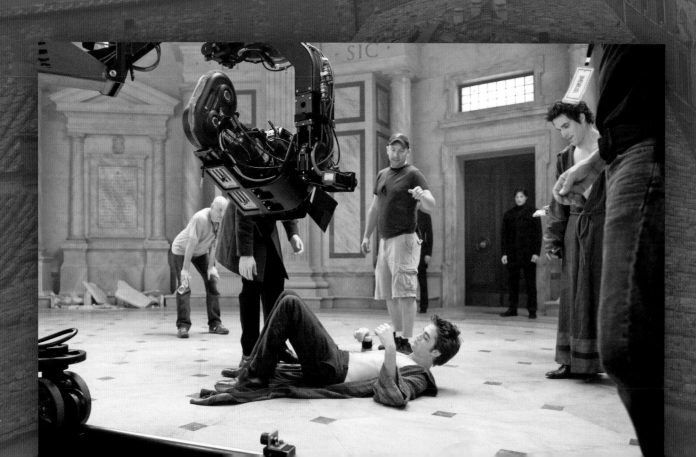

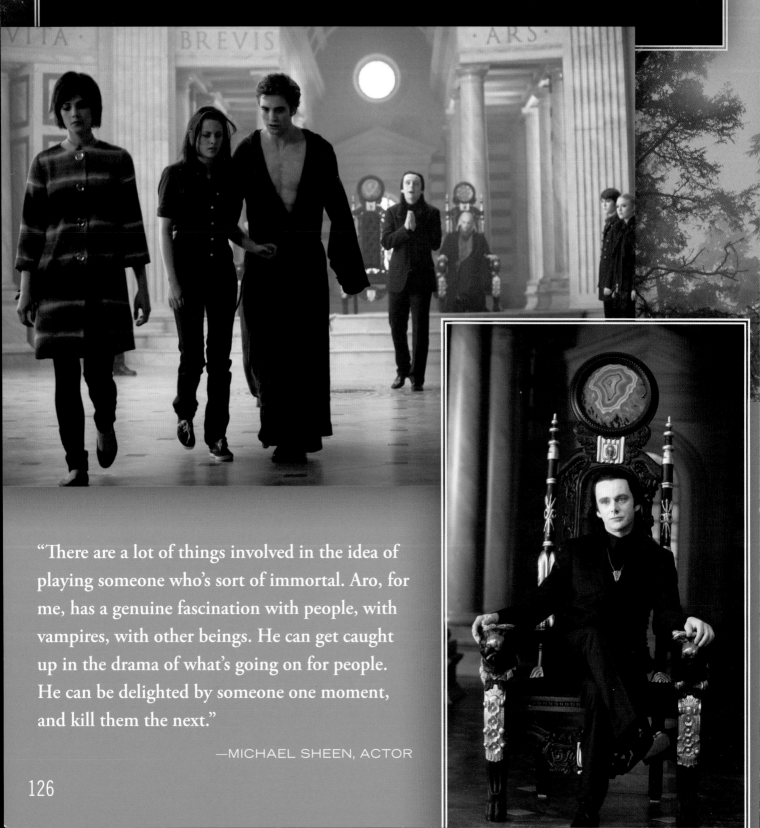

"All the vampires, especially the Volturi, seem very comfortable with their existence, but they see themselves as monsters. And when they see this human who says, 'I love this guy,' they all obviously want that, too. They want to believe that can happen. So, that curiosity, their fascination with that, is essentially what saves him."

—ROBERT PATTINSON, ACTOR

"There are a lot of things involved in the idea of playing someone who's sort of immortal. Aro, for me, has a genuine fascination with people, with vampires, with other beings. He can get caught up in the drama of what's going on for people. He can be delighted by someone one moment, and kill them the next."

—MICHAEL SHEEN, ACTOR

what was appropriate. Stephenie pointed out that Felix is a Volturi Guard, and his gift is fighting, so that would be enough of a challenge for Edward."

The stunt coordinator noted the idea was not to show an outlandish, superhero-type battle, that Edward was not a martial arts fighter looking to brawl. "Edward is like the average guy caught in a bad situation," Makaro said. "Much of the fight, it's Edward, Felix, and Demetri. For Bella, we tried to convey the feeling of a human being caught in the middle of a pack of vampires fighting."

There was wire work, but also an emphasis on hands-on fighting at vampire speed which, for *New Moon*, meant slow motion. "Slow motion was the main signature of the fight," Makaro explained. "We wanted to play this low and on the ground. They're not super flying around and smashing into walls, it was a lot more grabbing each other and breaking away and hitting each other."

The fight scene also would switch to different speeds, from the perspective of Bella watching the fight, to putting the audience in with the vampires as they fought. "We found if you sped up the [camera] speed, it would look silly," Makaro added. "We spent a lot of time figuring out what speeds were best for certain fight moves."

At one point, Edward's head gets smashed on the marble floor and his vampire skin appears to crack, along with the floor. It seems Edward is done for, but his wound suddenly heals. "I said to Chris, 'Isn't healing more of a wolf thing?'" MacLeod recalled. "And he said, 'Yeah, I'd better call Stephenie.' So he called Stephenie and got

her approval to crack and heal Edward's face! Any ideas or questions would always go through Stephenie, because she has the whole mythology in her head."

For the effect, Prime Focus created a CG floor and a CG crack effect on Edward's face. "It was a similar match-move effect to the diamond-skin effect, where the CG model [of the actor's face] is perfectly animated to the motion picture image," Pascarelli said.

Daniel Cudmore as Volturi guard member, Felix.

"ANY IDEAS OR QUESTIONS WOULD ALWAYS GO THROUGH STEPHENIE, BECAUSE SHE HAS THE WHOLE MYTHOLOGY IN HER HEAD."

Destiny

*Robert Pattinson as Edward Cullen and
Kristen Stewart as Bella Swan.*

As the summer months of postproduction rolled on, editor Peter Lambert worked with Chris Weitz on the final cut. "Editing a film is hard and absolutely subjective," Lambert noted. "One thing that's important is to maintain a freshness. We were only three weeks into the postproduction work and I'd seen each scene maybe twenty or thirty times, and an assembled version of the entire film perhaps half a dozen times. But every time I looked at it, I had to see it as if I were that audience member seeing the film for the first time."

Lambert also had to wrestle with an initial three-hour cut of the final film. "I was a little nervous when I had the first assembly. I know TWILIGHT fans will think, 'Three hours of Edward and Bella and Jacob, that would be heaven!' But the reality was it was too flabby, the pacing [was off]. But that sort of thing is inevitable in any first assembly, you're kind of flying blind when you're cutting it together. So we had to cut down the length. But it was never about cutting scenes, just cutting down the length of scenes for pacing. You have to rigorously go through and see what is essential. Chris was with me every day, we'd sit together and go through every moment of each scene, looking at all the alternatives of what had been shot.

"This is a movie with visual effects and action and horror, but it's really a love story, we're on an emotional journey with the

Part of Bella's dream.

Edward (Pattinson) explores Bella's room.

"The best way to do a personal job on a movie is to dream about it. Prepare for all possibilities. Have a very clear idea of the color palette. Achieve perfect communication with the director. And surround yourself with the best collaborators. With all of our possibilities and our idea of light, with that dream, we present our images."

—JAVIER AGUIRRESAROBE, DIRECTOR OF PHOTOGRAPHY

characters," Lambert added. "And Kristen, Taylor, and Robert were amazing, they were totally into their characters. In the dailies, with the different takes, you could see when they were getting into it, those moments of awareness. In early takes, you might sense they were thinking about hitting their mark, or speaking their lines, but then you'd see it happen—the nuances and awareness of what their character was feeling. My job as an editor is to be discreet, you don't want the editing to stand out. It's about finding the moments within the shots which work best for the performance."

> "THIS IS A MOVIE WITH VISUAL EFFECTS AND ACTION AND HORROR, BUT IT'S REALLY A LOVE STORY, WE'RE ON AN EMOTIONAL JOURNEY WITH THE CHARACTERS."

Bella loves the story of Romeo and Juliet *and so does her creator, Stephenie Meyer.*

Making a movie is like a traveling magic show that appears, conjures its illusions, and vanishes, leaving behind the imprint of its dreams upon the medium of film, and so it was with *The Twilight Saga: New Moon*. But, as a franchise, the studio could conjure anew, could return to an evolving world.

"It's heartbreaking to think that Volturi set won't exist forever, that it's not really made of marble and will be torn down," Gillian Bohrer reflected. "The whole filmmaking process is very temporary. When a production starts the crew becomes a real family, the actors become friends, and then everyone disperses. Their work lives on-screen, but the actual pieces that are put together for that period of time get torn down or recycled. But what's great about doing a franchise is we get to come back and do it again. Every book, thematically, has its own story. I like the fact that we have different directors, with different styles, on each movie. But the characters, and actors, are the same. Each movie feels unique, but is part of a whole."

As *New Moon* was in postproduction, *The Twilight Saga: Eclipse* was in the works and looking at a scheduled start of principal photography in August of 2009. "We are working on the script," Bohrer noted in June. "We only have a few new roles for casting, we already have half our locations. It's funny, *New Moon* has been a very different experience than *Twilight*. The time we spent scouting locations for *New Moon*, I spent looking for a director and working with Melissa on the script for *Eclipse*. So, while

"This movie, for me, has been redemptive. I had a difficult go on my last film, where I felt the movie was kind of taken away from me. This movie has been a joy in comparison and I've been able to make use of everything I've learned up to this point, and I've gotten the chance to work with some extraordinary people. Going in, I didn't realize the enthusiasm [of the fan base], and that was also inspiring. As Peter Lambert and I sat in the editing room, it gave me an added incentive. I don't think anyone knew there would be this degree of enthusiasm and that there would be this cyclonic snowball effect of books and films feeding on one another to make this amazing cultural moment."

—CHRIS WEITZ, DIRECTOR

Wyck's mind has been on *New Moon*, my mind has been on *Eclipse*. But what's fun about doing a franchise is you get multiple opportunities to build on what you're done in the past. *Twilight* was a good starting point. Our actors have done a phenomenal job. I can't wait to see where it goes next."

Summit president Erik Feig noted the studio's strategy was to have different directors for each film. "Each book has a central emotional quandary and scope, and we've tried to find the right director for each. *Twilight* is raw and real and Catherine Hardwicke was the first director I met with and the only director for that movie. *New Moon* has more complicated emotions, with bigger forces at work, and Chris Weitz was the director with the skill set to show that. On *Eclipse* the challenge is how do you visualize and show

"EACH MOVIE FEELS UNIQUE, BUT IS PART OF A WHOLE."

an audience that choice has consequences, that Bella is in a crucible of multiple decisions and options? Who can get that? David Slade. So, for each one of those movies, in terms of the central emotional quandary and the visual scope, we tried to find the right director, and I've been really happy with each one."

"In *Eclipse* you're back into narrative filmmaking," Wyck Godfrey added. "Now the stage has been set. The relationships and all the forces are aware of Bella and they're crashing in. . . . What's going to happen to Forks, to her family and friends?"

In the novel, NEW MOON ends with Edward and Bella facing those questions together. "Edward was here, with his arms around me," Bella thinks, drawing in a deep breath. "I could face anything as long as that was true."[10]

"I SQUARED MY SHOULDERS AND
WALKED FORWARD TO MEET
MY FATE, WITH MY DESTINY
SOLIDLY AT MY SIDE."[11]

NOTES

1: Stephenie Meyer, *New Moon* (New York: Megan Tingley Books, Little, Brown and Company, paperback edition, 2008), p. 283.

2: Ibid., p. 201.

3: Mark Cotta Vaz, *Twilight: The Complete Illustrated Movie Companion* (New York: Little, Brown and Company, 2008), p. 123.

4: Meyer, *New Moon* paperback, pp. 71–72.

5: "'Twilight' Sequel Loses Its Director," from "Arts, Briefly," compiled by Dave Itzkoff, *The New York Times*, December 9, 2008.

6: Meyer, *New Moon* paperback, p. 6.

7: James Harding, *The Pre-Raphaelites* (New York: Rizzoli International Publications, Inc., 1977), p. 5.

8: Stephenie Meyer, *Twilight* (New York: Megan Tingley Books, Little, Brown and Company, paperback edition, 2006), p. 124.

9: Meyer, *New Moon* paperback, p. 442.

10: Ibid., p. 563.

11: Ibid., p. 563.

All quotes from actors Kristen Stewart, Robert Pattinson, Taylor Lautner, Tyson Houseman, Chaske Spencer, Bronson Pelletier, and Michael Sheen are from the production's electronic press kits (and are edited for continuity). The author thanks Summit Entertainment for making this material available for this book.

ACKNOWLEDGMENTS

Many thanks to Chris Weitz, Erik Feig, and the entire *The Twilight Saga: New Moon* production team who gave of their time to be interviewed for this book.

My thanks go to Megan Tingley at Little, Brown and Company, who asked me to write it, and Erin Stein who deftly edited it. At Summit, Juliet Berman, executive assistant to Nancy Kirkpatrick, was indispensable in putting me in contact with the filmmakers. My brilliant agent, John Silbersack, helped get me going, and his assistant Emma Beavers was a delightful resource throughout.

A low bow and tip of the hat to: Dave Roker (assistant to Chris Weitz); Michael Lewis (agent for Javier Aguirresarobe); Lori C. Petrini, Niketa Roman, and Kip Larsen (Tippett Studio); and Allison Garfield (assistant to Bill Bannerman). And while I'm at it, my thoughts of appreciation fly out to Joe Monti and literary guru Bob Wyatt. My appreciation to Bettylu Sullivan Vaz, my mom, who expertly proofed the manuscript; love to padre and the whole family, and a special tip of the old chapeau to my brother Patrick, blogger extraordinaire, patron of the arts, and supreme resource for fact-checks on all literary matters. And here's a final shout-out to Mike Wigner, world's greatest bicycle messenger—Wig! It's that time again. Grab the usual table at Vesuvio's—it's a wrap.

Photo © Bruce Walters

AUTHOR'S CREDITS

Mark Cotta Vaz is the author of 27 books. He is the author of a number of *New York Times* bestsellers, including #1 bestselling *Twilight: The Complete Illustrated Movie Companion*, which also made the *USA Today* list of top 100 titles of 2008. He is currently working on the untold story of Pan American Airways.

Uncover the Secrets of twilight!

These two extraordinary books provide you with compelling looks behind the scenes of *Twilight*! *Twilight: The Complete Illustrated Movie Companion* has exclusive images and interviews with producers and set designers about the making of the film. *Twilight: Director's Notebook* is an intimate, first-person account of the entire process from groundbreaking director Catherine Hardwicke.

atom

www.atombooks.co.uk

www.stepheniemeyer.co.uk

The #1 Bestselling Books
That Started It All

And don't miss the Twilight Journals—
four journals featuring quotes from the books packaged
in a collectible tin—coming October 13, 2009!